Teachers' Problem Solving
A Casebook of Award-Winning Teaching Cases

TEACHERS' PROBLEM SOLVING

A Casebook of Award-Winning Teaching Cases

James M. Cooper, Editor

Winners of a National Competition Sponsored by the Commonwealth Center for the Education of Teachers

University of Virginia
James Madison University

Allyn and Bacon

Boston • London • Toronto • Sydney • Tokyo • Singapore

Series Editor: Virginia Lanigan
Series Editorial Assistant: Nicole DePalma
Marketing Manager: Ellen Mann
Prepress buyer: Linda Cox
Cover Administrator: Linda Knowles
Cover Designer: Suzanne Harbison

Copyright © 1995 by Allyn & Bacon
A Simon & Schuster Company
Needham Heights, Massachusetts 02194

Library of Congress Cataloging-in-Publication Data

Teachers' problem solving : a casebook of award-winning teaching cases
/ James M. Cooper, editor.
   p.   cm.
  "Winners of a national competition sponsored by the Commonwealth Center for the Education of Teachers, University of Virginia, James Madison University."
  ISBN 0-205-15203-1
  1. Teachers—Case studies. 2. Case method.   I. Cooper, James Michael, 1939– . II. James Madison University. Commonwealth Center for the Education of Teachers.
LB1775.T4176 1995
371.--dc20   94-12554
                                                    CIP

Printed in the United States of America

10 9 8 7 6 5 4 3 2 1   99 98 97 96 95 94

Credits:
page 12: "Strong Men" from *Collected Poems of Sterling A. Brown* selected by Michael S. Harper. Copyright 1932 by Harcourt Brace & Company. Copyright renewed 1960 by Sterling Brown. Reprinted by permission of HarperCollins Publishers Inc.

page 17: "Lift Every Voice and Sing" by J. Rosamond Johnson and James Weldon Johnson. Used by permission of Edward B. Marks Music Company.

CONTENTS

FOREWORD

This volume represents the fruits of national competition designed to encourage teachers, students of teaching, and college and university faculty to write stories about life in schools. These stories, or cases, describe moments in time as they unfold every day across the country.

Although the authors make no claims for the generalizability of the cases, it is difficult to read them without feeling like you have been there, wherever "there" happens to be. Indeed authenticity was one criterion upon which these cases were selected. No doubt the richness and diversity of the cultures the writers portray reinforces this feeling. Anyone who has taught school or spent time talking with teachers will recognize, sometimes with uncomfortable clarity, the problems described here. Those who are less familiar with the professional side of teaching are bound to walk away from discussions of these cases knowing the job is more interesting and complex than they thought.

The phrases "teaching with cases," "case-based teaching," "case-method instruction" are now part of the vernacular of teacher education. This volume does not settle the arguments about the meanings of these terms or the worth of such approaches to preparing teachers. Instead, the book and the competition that spawned it have broadened participation in the debates. More important to those teachers, would-be teachers, and teacher educators who pay the purchase price, the nine cases have been edited in a way that enhances their practical value.

Many people and organizations have helped finance the competition and the preparation of the book. These include: Nancy Forsyth, Virginia Lanigan, and Mylan Jaixen of Allyn & Bacon; David Imig of the

American Association of Colleges for Teacher Education; Gloria Chernay of the Association of Teacher Educators; and Sharon Robinson and Sylvia Seidel of the National Education Association's Center for Innovation. The Commonwealth Center for the Education of Teachers, sponsor of the competition, would never have undertaken this project were it not for the support of our friends in Richmond at the State Council of Higher Education for Virginia. We are grateful for the kindness and generosity these people have shown us.

The judges who cast critical eyes on the submissions and picked the nine winners deserve our appreciation: Dan Hallahan, Professor of Education, University of Virginia; Kim Lancaster, teacher, Bath County Elementary School; John McIntyre, Professor of Education, Southern Illinois University serving for the Association of Teacher Educators; Kay Merseth, Harvard University; Greta Morine-Dershimer, Professor of Education, University of Virginia; Virginia Richardson, Professor of Education, University of Arizona, serving for the American Association of Colleges for Teacher Education; Sharon Robinson, Center for Innovation, National Education Association; and Judy Shulman, Far West Laboratory for Educational Research and Development.

Denise Huffman, Gail Duggan, and Becky Burbach shuffled manuscripts, typed, and edited copy with great skill and good humor. We are thankful to have them as colleagues.

> Robert F. McNergney
> Professor and Director
> Commonwealth Center for the
>   Education of Teachers
> University of Virginia
> Charlottesville, Virginia

CASE AUTHORS

James M. Cooper is Commonwealth Professor in the Curry School of Education where he also served as Dean from 1984 to 1994. He received four degrees from Stanford University—two in history and two in education, including his Ph.D. in 1967. He taught junior and senior high school social studies for four years in Palo Alto, California. He has authored, co-authored, or edited twenty book chapters, twenty-eight journal articles, sixteen monographs, and seven books, including *Those Who Can, Teach; Kaleidoscope: Readings in Education;* and *Classroom Teaching Skills*. His books and articles address the areas of teacher education, supervision of teachers, microteaching, and teacher education program evaluation.

Robert F. McNergey left the faculty of the University of Minnesota in 1980 to come to the University of Virginia where he serves as Professor of Educational Studies and Director of the Commonwealth Center for the Education of Teachers. He has degrees from the University of Nebraska, University of Vermont, and Syracuse University. He taught public school and coached in Iowa and Vermont. He has coauthored one book, edited two, and is presently editing one and coauthoring another. McNergey's writing has appeared in the *Handbook of Research on Teacher Education, Educational Researcher, Journal of Teacher Education, The Washington Post,* and *The New York Times*. When Division K (Teaching and Teaching Education) was formed in the American Educational Research Association, he was appointed as its first secretary.

Gerald P. Speckhard is currently Professor of Education at Valparaiso University specializing in secondary education and where he also served fifteen years as Chair of the Education Department. He received his Ed.D. degree at the University of Colorado with graduate work also at the University of Wisconsin and Stanford University. Previous experience includes teaching secondary school mathematics in Houston and Denver. His recent research and publication interests are on at-risk students in the secondary schools.

Debra Eckerman Pitton, currently a member of the Education Department of Gustavus Adolphus College in St. Peter, Minnesota, received her Ph.D. from the University of North Texas in 1989. Previous experience includes secondary and middle school teaching in the areas of English, speech and theater. In addition to the use of case studies to facilitate teacher reflection, Dr. Pitton's areas of interest include multiculturalism, middle level education and communication skills for educators.

Jacqueline A. Stefkovich is an associate professor in the Department of Educational Leadership and Policy Studies in the College of Education at Temple University, Philadelphia, Pa. She began her career as a kindergarten teacher, worked as a guidance counselor in two public schools, and later assumed a position as the state director for guidance and counseling at the New Jersey Department of Education. Most recently she has worked at Research for Better Schools, the United States Department of Education's regional educational laboratory for the mid-Atlantic region. She hold an Ed.D. in Administration, Planning, and Social Policy from Harvard University and a J.D. from the University of Pennsylvania Law School.

Michael L. Silverman is currently an intern principal for the School District of Philadelphia. In the past, he has held positions in public schools as a Dean of Students and as Coordinator of Special Education. For fifteen years, he worked as a special education teacher in the cities of Philadelphia, Pennsylvania and Camden, New Jersey. He holds a B.S. degree in Special Education from Temple University and an M.Ed. in Special Education from Antioch College. Mr. Silverman is licensed as a school principal in the state of Pennsylvania.

Clayton Keller is an Assistant Professor and Program Coordinator of Special Education at the University of Minnesota, Duluth. After teaching students with behavior disorders in the public schools, he earned his doctorate in special education at the University of Virginia. His research interests include educators with disabilities and the integration of students with disabilities in general education classrooms. He also serves as the chair of The Council for Exceptional Children's Presidential Commission on Special Educators with Disabilities.

Joan Karp has a Ph.D. in special education from the University of Connecticut. An Associate Professor, she coordinates the Early Childhood Studies Program at the University of Minnesota, Duluth. Her most recent research is in the areas of the integration and inclusion of young children with disabilities in early childhood programs and of the ways professionals from health, education, and social services can work together on behalf of young children with disabilities.

Elizabeth Quintero is an Assistant Professor of Early Childhood/Elementary Education at the University of Minnesota, Duluth. Her doctorate, from New Mexico State University, was in Curriculum and Instruction with a major in Early Childhood Education and a minor in Bilingual Education. Her teaching, research, and service revolve around her interests in early education, family contexts of diverse cultural groups, family literacy, and biliteracy development.

Allan A. Glatthorn is professor of education at East Carolina University, where his research and teaching focus on issues of curriculum and supervision. He has been a high school teacher, principal, and supervisor; he was formerly on the faculty at the University of Pennsylvania and served for a year as acting director of the University of Alaska Fairbanks School of Education.

He is the author of fourteen professional books and numerous school textbooks. His most recent book, *The Quality Curriculum,* was published in 1994 by the Association for Supervision and Curriculum Development. He has served as a consultant to more than two hundred school systems, helping them develop curricula and implement differentiated models of teacher supervision.

After leaving her teaching position at Boston University's School of Management in 1992, where she had taught courses in organizational behavior and pedagogy, **Jan Wohlberg** expanded her training and consulting practice. As president of Hands-On Learning, Inc., she develops, writes, and facilitates cases and experiential exercises for college classrooms and organizations in the business and non-profit sectors. Her materials have been published in textbooks on management and communication, and many individual cases and exercises have been widely distributed for use in illustrating principles of participative management, values clarification, leadership issues, and human resources issues. They have been used in college courses as far ranging as psychology, sociology, principles of public relations, women's issues, counselling psychology, and organizational behavior. The most recent of her three books, *OB in Action: Cases and Exercises* (Boston: Houghton Mifflin Co., 1992), with co-author Scott Weighart, is a compilation of some of those cases and exercises which have proven most successful and popular. A fourth book is scheduled to be published by Houghton Mifflin in November, 1994.

Betty Hallenback received a B.A. in sociology and anthropology from Carleton College in 1982 and an M.Ed. in special education from the University of Virginia in 1985. She taught self-contained and resource special education classes in Virginia and Oregon for six years. She received her Ph.D. in special education from the University of Virginia in 1994 and is currently an assistant professor of special education at Utah State University.

Katherine M. Gehl earned her undergraduate degrees at the University of Notre Dame in French and government. She worked for the International Monetary Fund in Washington D.C. before attending Catholic University for a master's in secondary education. After student teaching in a Washington D.C. public school, Katherine returned to her family's business in Germantown, Wisconsin to build a marketing department for the company. She is sales and marketing manager for Gehl's Guernsey Farms, Inc., a national food and beverage manufacturer, and is currently pursuing an MBA in marketing and human resources at Northwestern University.

Cheryl Sandora, a former English teacher, is now a doctoral candidate in the Department of Instruction and Learning at the University of Pittsburgh. She is currently working both as a Graduate Research Assistant at the Learning Research and Development Center of the University of Pittsburgh and a Teaching Assistant in the Department of Instruction and Learning. Her research interests include teacher preparation, and reading and discussion.

Teachers' Problem Solving
A Casebook of Award-Winning Teaching Cases

INTRODUCTION: THE VALUE OF CASES IN TEACHER EDUCATION

JAMES M. COOPER & ROBERT F. McNERGNEY

Teacher education has been both the subject and object of reform efforts through the years—microteaching, simulations, competency-based teacher education, protocol materials, modular instruction, extended programs, field-based instruction, cooperative learning—to name but a few. Some of these reforms were structural in nature, that is, they addressed program length or organization. Others were instructionally oriented and provided different kinds of learning experiences. Despite such efforts, program organization remains largely impervious to lasting change; most teacher education instruction, other than clinical and field experiences, consists of lecture and discussion. Students are to learn a body of knowledge imparted by the instructor or by a textbook. The assumption is that prospective students will learn facts, concepts, principles, and theories related to teaching and will draw on that knowledge as needed when teaching.

One problem with this approach is that the knowledge a prospective teacher is to master is held separate or apart from the circumstances in which it is to be applied. In the language of the day people often speak of such knowledge as being "deconstructed" and "decontextualized." Prospective teachers are asked "to know in general" rather than "to

1

know and apply" in the context of a specific situation. For example, learning reinforcement principles in an educational psychology course well enough to pass a written examination, does not insure that a prospective teacher can (1) recognize situations that might warrant the use of positive or negative reinforcement in a classroom, and (2) apply reinforcement theory to change a student's behavior.

The emphasis in teacher education programs on acquiring knowledge instead of applying it often stimulates criticism that programs are too "theoretical" and not sufficiently "practical." As others have observed over the years, the problem is not that programs are too theoretical, but that theory has not been related to real circumstances to help prospective teachers interpret what is happening and to guide their actions. Student teaching and field experiences in school classrooms are usually cited by teacher education students as the most valuable parts of their programs precisely because in these experiences they learn how to think and act like teachers. Teacher education programs need to capitalize on such experiences. The use of case methods may help students forge connections between knowledge and practice, and in doing so, revitalize the pedagogy of teacher education programs.

What Are Cases?

Lee Shulman (1992) defines a case as a narrative story containing a set of events that unfold over time in a particular place. Teaching cases, as used in teacher education, are original narratives and descriptions of teaching that have been constructed specifically for a teacher's education. They can be short (a paragraph or so) or long (fifty or more pages); most are based on fact. To call something a case, Shulman argues, is to make a theoretical claim that the narrative is an instance of a larger class, that is, it is a "case-of-something." This distinguishes cases from simple anecdotes or vignettes that do not imply a larger typology. Shulman goes on to say, however, that a case collected for one purpose need not be limited to that purpose, but could be used as a case of something else if appropriate. In other words, cases may be rich enough to be instances of more than one typology or category.

Cases have been used extensively in business, law, medicine, and clinical psychology. Instructors use cases in these fields in markedly different ways. In law, for example, instructors teach legal principles via cases. Students study court cases and decisions rendered by judges to learn foundations of judicial reasoning. Although legal decisions can be and are modified or even overturned by subsequent court rulings, past decisions become precedents for future decisions. Thus, over time, cases accumulate into a body of knowledge that guides legal practice.

In business education, instructors use cases quite differently. Business cases are used to teach students how to analyze problems and to determine appropriate courses of action. The cases used almost always represent actual problems that have confronted managers, and they are carefully constructed to provoke discussion and analysis.

The pedagogy used in legal and business education differs as well. In law schools instructors question Socratically to lead students to predetermined right answers. In business schools, case instructors question to encourage students to think analytically with the possibility of arriving at different conclusions. Interaction among business students is promoted and encouraged by the instructor.

A Knowledge Base for Teachers

For years educational researchers have explored concepts of more and less effective teaching to guide the preparation of teachers. They have sought characteristics such as personalities or attitudes that differentiate effective teachers from ineffective ones. They have studied teacher behaviors that seem to cause students to learn. The results of this work represent what might be characterized as the foundation of the knowledge base for teachers—a base upon which teachers can begin to construct pedagogical decisions and professional judgments. The principles of teaching and learning that have emerged from this research tradition offer direction to teachers, but they cannot be applied religiously to yield teaching success. Although there is a sameness or routinization of teaching wherever and whenever it occurs, the uniqueness and complexity of teachers' situations militate against such action.

Some principles govern good teaching, but teachers must decide how to apply them. N. L. Gage (1978) asserts that using the science of teaching to achieve practical ends requires artistry—"the artistry that enters into knowing when to follow the implications of the laws, generalizations, and trends, and especially, when **not** to, and how to combine two or more laws or trends in solving a problem." (p. 18)

Some educators argue, however, that teachers do not operate from a scientifically derived set of principles or theories, but rely instead on strategies for practice based on their past experiences. These experiences are organized and accessible in teachers' minds, but are also subject to continual modification. This line of reasoning contends that teachers' thoughts, memories of patterns of events, or conceptual frameworks, influence teaching decisions, in effect swamping any scientifically derived principles acquired in college classes.

Clark and Lampert (1986) take a slightly different tack by asserting that teachers' knowledge is (1) contextual, that is, situation specific;

(2) interactive, both informing and being informed by interactions with students; and (3) speculative, since much of teachers' work involves uncertainty. Principles in teaching exist, but how and when they are applied must be determined by the teacher based on situation specific circumstances.

The Case for Cases

If students of teaching are to think like teachers, maybe they need practice. Maybe they need opportunities to encounter real teaching problems in the safety and security of simulated situations—situations where they can retrieve principles of teaching and learning and try them out without damaging themselves and others in the process. Maybe cases can provide such opportunities. Merseth (1991), drawing from experiences in other fields and some preliminary work in education, identifies several benefits one might expect from applying case methods to teacher education programs.

1. Cases help students develop skills of critical analysis and problem solving. Well-constructed cases of teaching experiences can help students observe closely, make inferences, identify relationships, and articulate organizing principles. As Merseth states: "Cases send a powerful message that teaching is complex, contextual, and reflexive." (p. 16)
2. Case-based instruction encourages reflective practice and deliberate action by permitting students to discuss and choose from among competing interpretations advanced by one another. This process is indicative of Donald Schon's and John Dewey's vision of "reflection-in-action."
3. Cases help students analyze and make decisions in complex situations that may not be a perfect match between theory and practice. Merseth makes two points regarding this benefit of using cases: they bring "chunks of reality" into the classroom, and they expose students to settings and contexts that would normally not be available.
4. Case-based instruction involves students in their own learning. Students cannot sit back passively as they might in a lecture situation, but must share an active responsibility in the learning that occurs. Moreover, case-based instruction tends to generate lively and engaging discussions. Students have the opportunity to begin assuming the role of teacher as they express their own knowledge, values, opinions, and interpretations about teaching.

5. The case method encourages the creation of a community of learners. By taking responsibility for their own learning as well as contributing to the learning of others, students learn to work together in teams.

Sykes and Bird (1992) and Grossman (1992), drawing on research by Spiro, et al. (1987), conclude that case methods may be best suited for learning in areas that could be called "ill-structured domains." Such domains are characterized by ambiguity; they are domains in which relevant knowledge is not organized to fit a particular situation. As Grossman states: "The value of cases for teacher education lies in their potential to represent the messy world of practice, to stimulate problem solving in a realm in which neither the problem nor the solution is clear." (p. 237) Teaching is nothing if not an "ill-structured domain." Every event unfolds differently, and teachers must orchestrate a myriad of factors to encourage learning. Spiro and his colleagues (1988) state:

In ill-structured domains, general principles will not capture enough of the structured dynamics of cases; increased flexibility in responding to highly diverse new cases comes increasingly from reliance on reasoning from precedent cases. Thus, examples/cases cannot be assigned the ancillary status of merely illustrating abstract principles (and then being discardable); the cases are key—examples are necessary, and not just nice. (p. 379)

One of the most compelling arguments for using cases to prepare teachers is that they relate good stories. Stories are powerful and easier to remember than decontextualized information, and they seem to "fit" with teachers' ways of organizing their knowledge of teaching.

While advocates for the use of case methods in teacher education are growing in number, others remain skeptical. The skeptics point out, rightfully so, that virtually no research evidence exists regarding the efficacy of case methods in teacher education. Sykes and Bird, citing a small literature, report that this work suggests that a case curriculum is inefficient in transmitting codified knowledge useful to complex practice; that single cases fail to help students see underlying issues and develop useful principles and generalizations; and that case discussions substitute analysis of others' experiences for students' own experiential learning.

Despite limitations, case-method teaching in teacher education grows in popularity. We need research on case methods to move ahead, but it will not be conducted unless pioneer teacher educators and teachers are developing and using cases. With this volume we hope to encourage the forward movement.

The Role of the Commonwealth Center in Case-Method Education

The Commonwealth Center for the Education of Teachers is a joint enterprise of the University of Virginia and James Madison University. Funded by the General Assembly of the Commonwealth of Virginia in 1988, the Center has both research and program improvement in teacher education as its central mission. One of the major programs of the Center has been to develop and study both written and videotaped cases as they are used in teacher education programs. The Center has encouraged reform of teacher education by supporting the institutionalization of recent innovations in case-method teaching that promise to affect how we educate and evaluate teachers.

Center work has been based on the assumption, as we note above, that teacher education has often encouraged teachers to *acquire* knowledge but not to *use* it to solve problems of teaching and learning. Professors lecture, discuss theory in the abstract, give multiple-choice tests, and all too frequently reinforce the belief that schools of education have little or nothing to offer serious professionals. In contrast, case-method teaching seems to narrow the gap between theory and practice by engaging students of teaching in real-life problems of schools.

The Center has pursued several lines of inquiry simultaneously. First, to encourage the development of cases, the Center sponsored a national case-writing competition for use in preservice teacher education courses. The Center staff assembled an expert board of reviewers, and solicited manuscripts by way of national publications read by teachers, administrators, and higher education personnel. Thirty-seven manuscripts concentrating on problems in the middle grades were received from across the country. Each reviewer read every manuscript and rated it according to its authenticity, possibilities for interpretation, and attention to the cultural diversity that characterizes our society. The nine top-rated manuscripts were selected for publication in this volume. Each winning author received a cash prize.

In one way, then, this volume differs from other casebooks with which we are familiar because it is the result of a national writing competition. It differs in another way: other casebooks have predetermined categories or classifications to guide the solicitation of cases. Because this book was planned as a compilation of the winning cases in the competition, we did not wish to dampen interest in participating by tightly circumscribing categories for submission of manuscripts. Our intent was not to provide a casebook illustrating certain aspects of teaching, such as classroom management or moral dilemmas. Instead we wished to stimulate interest in case-based teacher education, to make available well-written cases for use in teacher education courses, and to showcase the winners of the national case-writing competition.

Second, the Commonwealth Center established a national invitational team case competition involving preservice teachers. In May of 1992, with help from Allyn & Bacon, the American Association of Colleges for Teacher Education, the Association of Teacher Educators, and the National Education Association's Center for Innovation, the Commonwealth Center sponsored the first invitational team case competition for prospective teachers. Teams from the College of St. Rose, Florida State University, Hampton University, University of Minnesota, and the University of Pittsburgh met for three days at the University of Virginia in Charlottesville and demonstrated their case- analysis skills before a board of judges composed of nationally recognized experts in the fields of teaching, school administration, education, arts and sciences, business, law, and journalism (Commonwealth Center for the Education of Teachers, 1992).

If interest remains high, the Center will continue to sponsor the team competition each spring. Our intent is to make the competition an annual affair and to involve in-service teachers not only as judges and interrogators but as models who demonstrate best practice.

Third, we are in the process of describing the content of teams' case analyses. By using the computer program Ethnograph, we can identify patterns of thinking about the issues most salient in a case. This allows us to examine the perceived relevance of various actors' perspectives, the use of professional knowledge, and teaching actions deemed desirable by neophytes and experts. These early studies should help us understand how inexperienced teachers think about classroom problems, how they interact to resolve such problems, and how they might be encouraged to move toward more pedagogically mature ways of thinking and behaving.

Fourth, with assistance from the Hitachi Foundation, the Commonwealth Center is in the process of producing videotaped cases on teaching and learning in multicultural classrooms across the nation. These cases are designed to help teachers recognize teaching problems and opportunities, discern values that drive the actions of teachers and students, recognize relevant professional knowledge, forecast teaching actions, and speculate on the consequences of such actions (Herbert, 1991).

The videotapes are supplemented with (1) written teaching notes that provide directions for classroom instructors, and (2) multiple philosophical critiques written by experts on teaching and learning that communicate a range of acceptable teaching actions. Allyn & Bacon will publish and distribute these prototypical videotaped cases. This project will expand to include other types of classrooms and other philosophical analyses.

Fifth, Commonwealth Center staff are working with Curry School of Education faculty and faculty at other institutions of higher education in Virginia to institutionalize case-method teaching in extant teacher education programs. If it is going to last, we believe reform must begin at home. At our own institution we have begun to use case-based teaching throughout our five-year teacher education program. The first professional education course students take offers an excellent opportunity to familiarize students with case methods. Program faculty teach students again with case methods, although not exclusively, in each succeeding year of the professional program.

Although we prohibit University of Virginia students from competing, we also involve them in the national invitational team case competition, as program planners, guides, and observers. Our students occupy a special vantage point from which to view case-method teaching and learning.

Sixth, the Commonwealth has provided seed money to stimulate other institutions to commit to the use of cases in their teacher education programs. During the 1990–92 school years the Commonwealth Center for the Education of Teachers provided a total of $48,000 to 12 Virginia institutions through a mini-grant competition designed to stimulate the production of cases for use in teacher education. Those who won grants formed the nucleus of the Center's League of Innovative Programs. We shall continue the mini-grant program to provide seed money to other organizations outside the League to integrate case-based teaching into their preparation programs.

Future Directions

Like Kauffman (1993) and his colleagues, we are enthusiastic about case-method education, but we do not view it as a panacea for the ills of teacher education. Case-method teaching seems promising for some people for some objectives, but not for everyone for all purposes. We need to face some important issues as we try to use cases and understand their effects. For instance, can we integrate cases within programs to change demonstrably the form and function of those programs? If not, we may have yet another interesting instructional technique, but one that fails to make any appreciable change in the system. Without such systemic change, case-method teaching is likely to go the way of other so-called innovations. That cases hold some promise for use in areas other than teacher education—for example, school administrator preparation—encourages us about their potential staying power.

There is as yet no single commonly accepted strategy for case-method teaching, nor is there likely to be any time soon. We can be grateful for this period of experimentation and take advantage of the time to continue to explore multiple methods of developing, teaching with, and evaluating case methods.

It seems that if many people with interests in case-method teaching can continue to share ideas, we stand a better chance of making headway than if any of us were to go it alone. The support we have received from the American Association of Colleges for Teacher Education (AACTE), from the Association of Teacher Educators, the National Education Association, Allyn & Bacon, and from other professionals around the country is encouraging. We all need the kind of interaction that problems of case-method teaching seem to generate if we are to sharpen our notions of what constitutes the reasonable resolution of teaching and learning problems. Although hard-and-fast "answers" to problems rarely present themselves, there are few if any relativists in our business. We need to learn to formulate and communicate outcomes to case problems that are defensible and to make them public. When we can do so in a representational situation like a case, we will have begun to help real people do the same in real time and in real-life situations.

REFERENCES

Clark, C., & Lampert, M. (1986). The study of teacher thinking: Implications for teacher education. *Journal of teacher education* 37 (5): 27–31.

Commonwealth Center for the Education of Teachers (1992, spring/summer). Center hosts first national team competition in case methods. *Commonwealth Center News*, 4(2), 1–2.

Gage, N. L. (1978). The scientific basis of the art of teaching. New York: Teacher's College Press.

Grossman, P. L. (1992). Teaching and learning with cases. In J. H. Shulman (ed.), *Case methods in teacher education*. New York: Teacher's College Press.

Herbert, J. M. (1991, fall/winter). Grant emphasizes multicultural education. *Commonwealth Center News*, 4(1), 1.

Kauffman, J. M., Mostert, M. P., Nuttycombe, D. G., Trent, S. C., & Hallahan, D. P. (1993). *Managing classroom behavior: A reflective case-based approach*. Boston: Allyn & Bacon.

Merseth, K. K. (1991). The case for cases in teacher education. Washington, DC: American Association for Higher Education and the American Association of Colleges for Teacher Education.

Shulman, L. S. (1992). Toward a pedagogy of cases. In J. H. Shulman (ed.), *Case methods in teacher education*. New York: Teacher's College Press.

Spiro, R. J., Vispoel, W. P., Schmitz, J. G., Samarapungavan, A., & Boerger, A. E. (1987). Knowledge acquisition for application: Cognitive flexibility and transfer in complex domains. In B. C. Britton (ed.), *Executive control processes* (pp. 177–199). Hillsdale, NJ: Erlbaum.

Spiro, R. J., Coulson, R. L., Feltovich, P. J., & Anderson, D. K. (1988). Cognitive flexibility theory: Advanced knowledge acquisition in ill-structured domains. In *Tenth annual conference of the cognitive science society* (pp. 375–383). Hillsdale, NJ: Erlbaum.

Sykes, G., & Bird, T. (1992). Teacher education and the case idea. In G. Grant (ed.), *Review of research in education*, 18. Washington, DC: American Educational Research Association.

WHITE TEACHER—BLACK SCHOOL

KATHERINE M. GEHL

ABSTRACT

*One of the most talked about trends in American schools today is the imple-
mentation of an Afrocentric curriculum or inclusion of some Afrocentric materials in a traditional curriculum. What is Afrocentric education, and what
does it offer of value to today's student and teacher? What also are the
attendant difficulties in its implementation? In this case study, the protago-
nist, Gina Harris, confronts these issues in her student teaching.*

*Gina is a young white student teacher in a predominantly black school in
inner-city America, who initially approaches her job with optimism and
purpose. However, she begins to experience her first doubts with the presentation of an emotionally charged poetry reading at an all-school assembly. The
poem paints a picture of the oppression of African-Americans by the Euro-
American majority. Gina is moved by the poem and accepts the historical truth
of its message. At the same time, she wonders what the educational effects of
this poem are and whether it affects her legitimacy as a white teacher in a
black school. These questions resurface several times in the case as Gina
discusses her thoughts with her cooperating teacher and her fellow student
teachers. She struggles with these issues on both an emotional and theoretical
basis, finding that there are no easy answers to the question of what curriculum should be taught in our American schools. Readers of this case will find*

themselves presented with dilemmas that encompass practical and theoretical aspects of curriculum choice and education in a cross-cultural context.

White Teacher—Black School

An All-School Assembly—Central Middle School
   Gina Harris sat with her ninth-grade French class in the first assembly for Black History Month at Central Middle School. Everyone stood for the U. S. National Anthem. Then Mr. Smith, an African-American teacher, recited:

STRONG MEN

> They dragged you from homeland
> They chained you in coffles,
> They huddled you spoon-fashion in filthy hatches
> They sold you to give a few gentlemen ease.
>
> They broke you in like oxen
> They scourged you,
> They branded you,
> They made your women breeders,
> They swelled your numbers with bastards
> They taught you the religion they disgraced.
>
> You sang:
>   Keep a-inchin' along
>   Lak a po'inch worm . . .
>
> You sang:
>   Bye and bye
>   I'm gonna lay down dis heaby load . . .
>
> You sang:
>   Walk togedder, chillen,
>   Dontcha git weary . . .
>
> The strong men keep a-comin' on
> The strong men git stronger.

They point with pride to the roads you built for them,
They ride in comfort over the rails you laid for them.
They put hammers in your hands
And said—Drive so much before sundown.

You sang:
　　Ain't no hammah
　　In dis lan'
　　Strikes lak mine, bebby.
　　Strikes lak mine.

They cooped you in their kitchens,
They penned you in their factories,
They gave you the jobs that they were too good for,
They tried to guarantee happiness to themselves
By shunting dirt and misery to you.

You sang:
　　Me an' muh baby gonna shine, shine
　　Me an' muh baby gonna shine,
　　　　The strong men keep a-comin' on
　　　　The strong men git stronger . . .

They bought off some of your leaders
You stumbled, as blind men will . . .
They coaxed you, unwontedly sof-voiced . . .
You followed a way
Then laughed as usual.
They heard the laughter and wondered;
Uncomfortable;
Unadmitting a deeper terror . . .

　　The strong men keep a-comin' on
　　Gittin' stronger . . .

What from the slums
Where they have hemmed you,
What, from the tiny huts
They could not keep from you—
What reaches them
Making them ill at ease, fearful?
Today they shout prohibition at you
"Thou shalt not this"

"Thou shalt not that"
"Reserved for whites only"
You laugh.

One thing they cannot prohibit—
    The strong men . . . coming on
    The strong men gittin' stronger.
    Strong men . . .
    Stronger

—Sterling A. Brown

"Us, them; us, them" kept running through Gina Harris's mind even as Dr. Howard, the invited speaker, urged students to consider medicine as a career.

The assembly seemed to stir the pride of the African-American students, but it left Gina feeling unsettled. Some people would have said this was predictable. Although Gina had eagerly anticipated student teaching at Central, an inner-city school with a predominantly African-American population, it had, at least on the surface, nothing in common with her own background. She had grown up in a small, midwestern town. She did attend a public school; but, in her prosperous rural community, public school wasn't much like the cash-strapped Central. French was her favorite class in high school, and she went on to specialize in it at McCauley College, a private institution with a predominantly white, middle-class student body.

So the Central assignment seemed at odds with Gina's background, and, in fact, many of her friends had tried to convince her that she just wouldn't fit in and that it might even be dangerous for her to go there. But Gina brushed this aside. She loved French, and she knew she'd love teaching. She also was interested in the current trend toward Afrocentric education in this city's schools, and, in preparation for coming to Central, she already had spent many hours preparing a unit on French West Africa, trying to link cultural studies with the language. The cooperating teacher, Mr. James Sanders, a young, African-American member of the Central staff, welcomed Gina to the school in a manner that made her feel very comfortable. He had an outstanding reputation, and Gina was quite happy with her placement.

The poetry reading at the assembly, however, caused the first doubts to creep in. She could be considered one of the oppressive "they" featured in the poem. Gina started to think that maybe student teaching at this school wouldn't be as easy as she'd supposed.

A Student-Teaching Seminar—McCauley College

That afternoon, Gina went to her Wednesday student-teaching seminar. Here, all the student teachers got together with their professor to discuss, complain, ask questions, even cry if necessary, and generally analyze their experiences. Class started as usual with Dr. Gilbert asking, "So how's everybody doing? Any questions, problems, comments?" Gina waited for the other students to speak first, until Dr. Gilbert finally said, "Gina, we haven't heard from you much today. Have you been teaching?"

"Well, yes, I taught my first lesson last Friday, and this week I've been teaching two every day. It's really fun, and there haven't been any real problems. We've actually talked about my taking over one class beginning next week."

"That's fine if you feel ready," rejoined Dr. Gilbert, "but I want to reiterate for all of you, not just Gina, that it is very important not to take too much responsibility too soon. It doesn't reflect badly on you if you need a little more time. Sometimes cooperating teachers push their students into taking over too quickly. So don't be afraid to say you're not ready at this point."

Gina perked up again, "Oh, I really do think that I'm ready. I don't mean that it won't be difficult, but to tell you the truth it can get kind of boring sitting there watching all day long. I do think the kids seem real subdued with me compared to with Mr. Sanders, but he and this other teacher were telling me that that would just take a little time. What I'm actually concerned about doesn't have to deal exactly with my teaching. . . . You know because it's Black History Month, we're having all kinds of assemblies, at least one a week." Other students nod in agreement because it's much the same at their schools. "I really like them, and, in fact, I feel like I'm more interested in them than the students are and even perhaps more than my cooperating teacher. I think it's great to celebrate their culture like this. But today something happened. . . . I'm not criticizing it or anything, just wondering about it."

Gina went on to describe the recitation of the poem, *Strong Men*. "I really liked the poem; it's very truthful, and that man did a great job of interpreting it. But, what I'm wondering is, for example, if all of the students, being African-American, are supposed to identify with the 'us' in the poem, and they should, of course, because the purpose is for them to feel that they are strong in spite of all the oppression. But then, am I or any other white person in the audience, also necessarily supposed to identify with the 'they'?"

Dr. Gilbert turns the question to the class for comments, as is her custom. "Well, what do you all think?" Students generally sympathize with Gina, asserting that they too would feel uncomfortable in such a situation. One student categorically states that there should be no place in public schools for such inflammatory materials. Gina counters, "Well, I didn't mean to suggest they meant it to be inflammatory. I think the administration just wants to allow them to see reflections of their own culture in their school. It's only fair; but I just don't know what the real effects are of this kind of material. And what about the white teachers in a school like this?"

Angie, another student teaching in a primarily black school responds, "I really don't think it should be that big of a deal. People make it seem as if black kids don't learn like white kids or something. As far as I'm concerned, I'm a teacher, they are students; and I don't care whether they're black, white, or purple."

Gina persists, "But is that really fair to them? After all, we're always talking about meeting the psychological needs of our students. Is it possible to do that while ignoring something that defines a large part of their experience? What about when I use African-American literature in my classes? I have a whole series of poems and stories that I've already picked out."

The students don't come up with any real "answers" to Gina's questions. When 6:00 arrives, Dr. Gilbert breaks in, "Well, I'm not surprised that these issues are coming up. There aren't any pat answers to these difficulties, and I'm sure that we'll discuss this subject many times this semester. But something that you should remember is that you have a right to be there, just as any African-American teacher has a right to teach in a predominantly white school. I'm not saying that these issues don't come up or that they're not difficult issues, but you can't take it personally."

A Black National Anthem?

So Gina heads for home to work on the next day's lessons, still troubled by the day's occurrences. A couple of times on Thursday and Friday, she tried to convince herself to bring it up with James, just to see what he thought. But even though she was, in every other instance, very comfortable with him, she felt funny about talking so specifically about black versus white. So nothing was said; and, since there were no more assemblies that week, Gina didn't directly confront the issue again.

Since Gina lived pretty far away from Central, she always came in early to beat the traffic. She didn't mind too much since it gave her a chance to review everything she had planned for the day. Even though she was relatively at ease teaching her lessons, she still wouldn't dream of doing it without a lot of rehearsal in her head. Sitting at the one teacher's desk in the room, which James had generously said "is more your desk than mine for this semester," she happened to see in the trash can next to the desk some memos from the front office. She didn't have a mailbox, so she didn't get her own. Instead, she pulled these out of the trash. There were the predictable reminders to get the attendance in by third period and to watch the halls between classes to try to move the students to class a bit faster, and there was also a memo directing the teachers to write the Black National Anthem on the board. The principal was asking all teachers to go over it with their students before the next assembly on Friday because they were planning to sing it at that time.

DATE: February 10, 1990
TO: All Teachers
FROM: Mrs. Menor, Principal
RE: Black National Anthem

During the coming week I would ask you to write the Black National Anthem on the board and take the time to go over it with each one of your classes. We will be singing it at some of our upcoming assemblies for Black History Month, and it is important that each and every student knows it. Thank you, teachers.

LIFT EV'RY VOICE AND SING

Lift ev'ry voice and sing
Till earth and heaven ring.
Ring with the harmonies of Liberty;
Let our rejoicing rise
High as the list'ning skies,
Let it resound loud as the rolling sea.
Sing a song full of the faith that the dark past has taught us,
Sing a song full of the hope that the present has brought us.
Facing the rising sun of our new day begun,
Let us march on till victory is won.

Stony the road we trod,
Bitter the chast'ning rod.
Felt in the days when hope unborn had died;
Yet with a steady beat,

Have not our weary feet
Come to the place for which our fathers sighed?
We have come over a way that with tears has been watered,
We have come, treading our path through the blood of the
    slaughtered,
Out from the gloomy past,
Till now we stand at last
Where the white gleam of our bright star is cast.

God of our weary years,
God of our silent years,
Thou who has brought us thus far on the way;
Thou who has by Thy might
Led us into the light.
Keep us forever in the path, we pray.
Lest our feet stray from the places, our God, where we
    met Thee,
Lest our hearts, drunk with the wine of the world, we
    forget Thee,
Shadowed beneath thy hand,
May we forever stand,
True to our God
True to our native land.

Words by JAMES WELDON JOHNSON
Music by ROSAMOND JOHNSON

A Black National Anthem? Gina had never heard of such a thing, and the words written out on the memo didn't ring a bell either. And why was this in the trash? Why hadn't James mentioned it to her? And, the biggest question, how was she going to present this to her third period class, the one class that she was taking over completely today?

An Uncomfortable Discussion

It wasn't until lunch that Gina had a chance to bring this up with Mr. Sanders. They almost always ate lunch with James's best friend on the teaching staff, Andrew Jeffries, whom Gina had come to admire in the three weeks since coming to Central. He was about her age and re-minded her of her best friend from high school. Andrew was the one who told her that the reason her kids were so quiet with her was because they weren't used to seeing a young white woman try to teach them. He told her not to worry, that he talked to some of the kids and that they really did like her. Gina always looked forward to getting his perspective on her problems in the classroom.

This day, Andrew was complaining about the number of assemblies this year. He wanted to know how the administration always seemed to know exactly when he was planning a test so that they could stick an assembly in at the same time. Andrew's thoughts saved Gina from having to bring up the subject of the anthem herself. "Hey, Gina, did you see the memo about the Black National Anthem?" he asked. "Yes, I meant to ask you about that, James," said Gina, hoping that he wouldn't ask her where she saw it. "I'm kind of unsure about teaching that. I mean, I'm a little embarrassed to say it, but I had never heard of the Black National Anthem until I read the memo, and I'm wondering how seriously the kids are going to take it, I mean . . . with me teaching them about something I don't know." Gina was somewhat surprised by James's response when he suggested that she should just skip it. "Everybody already knows it anyway."

While Gina thought that that might work in this particular case, she didn't want to continue to ignore the insecurity that she had begun to feel as a white teacher addressing Afrocentric curricula. "Well, that might be okay this time, but what about the next time? I would like to know what you think. Don't you think the students might find it a little strange having me teach them the Black National Anthem?" In the discussion that followed, Gina and James decided that she should go ahead and teach it in third period to see how it went. This being decided, Gina felt that now was her chance to bring up her questions about the poem.

"There's another thing that I've been wondering about in this whole issue of Afrocentric education. Before I came here I really discounted those people who said I wouldn't be able to be an effective teacher here."

"Who said that?" Andrew broke in.

"Well, just some of my friends, really. And, I still think that's ridiculous. I really like teaching here, and I don't think it's made one bit of difference that, for example, I went to a high school that was very different than here. When I started reading about the reforms in education using Afrocentric curricula, I felt right away that it was a sound idea. It just makes sense to me that the experience of African-Americans should be part of the curriculum. It's kind of similar to what has been done to women—they've been underrepresented in the standard curriculum. But it's still not really a clear-cut issue, and I don't really know all that much about it. I'm just wondering, for example, about the effects of using things that seem somewhat, well, anti-white. It seems kind of contrary to the kind of society we should have. And yet, it is factual that what white people did to African-Americans in this country naturally would make lots of African-American historical writings lean in that direction. What made me think about all this is that poem from last week's assembly, *Strong Men*. I really liked the poem—it was very moving. But the thing I'm wondering is, if the students are all supposed to identify with the 'us' in the poem, am I necessarily supposed to identify with the 'they'?"

James interrupted, "Well, of course you are. The 'they' means white people."

"I know that, but what I'm saying is that it seems that the students here are supposed to be encouraged by the idea talked about in the poem that, despite all the oppression, they are strong, and they never buckled under. I can see why that's good. But I wasn't here as part of the 'they.' I'm not saying I don't recognize that it was white people who committed those crimes, but are the students, in the process of identifying with the 'us,' now going to identify me, or any other white teacher, or for that matter the three white students in this school, with the 'they'?"

"Of course they are. They understand what the poem is saying. You can't expect us to just pretend it never happened," said James.

The conversation wasn't going well at all from Gina's point of view. "I don't want to pretend it never happened either, not at all. I just want to know what it means for me as a teacher here and for my students. I'm not saying I didn't like it. I don't know exactly what I think. Do you see what I mean?"

"Well, it doesn't mean people are going to blame you; it's just factual material," said James.

Finally, Andrew broke in, "I see your point, Gina. James, she's not saying it's wrong. You could see why it could make her uncomfortable, can't you?"

Gina quickly rejoined, "Well, it's no big deal. It's just something that is interesting to think about. To tell you the truth, right now I'm more worried about how I'm going to handle seventh period today. Do you think I should forget about using that short paragraph until they've had a couple more days of homework on the verbs alone?"

Walking back to her classroom after lunch, Gina was almost sorry that she had brought the subject up. She felt like James had taken it as a challenge when she just wanted to get their opinions on it. In any case, it wasn't mentioned again at lunch or any other time.

A Challenge in the Classroom

Mr. Sanders taught the first and second classes on Wednesday mornings, for which Gina was grateful, because she intended to watch how he presented the anthem to guide her own teaching in third period. She didn't get many ideas, however, because he didn't make a big deal of it. He waited until the end of class to talk about it, and at that point there wasn't much time left. He had the kids read through it with him, and then class was over. Gina realized that it really shouldn't be that difficult.

Her next class was a challenge from the start. Gina started to wonder if it had been a good idea to spend so much time trying to get Russell Bellam to improve his attendance. He was a very bright student, one of the brightest around, Gina thought, but he just didn't apply himself; and on this particular day, he seemed intent on disrupting the class. Gina had found that ignoring him usually was the most effective way to get him to calm down. But, when he started making fun of one of the other students who had troubles pronouncing the new vocabulary, Gina couldn't ignore him anymore. She moved him to a seat in the back of the room, by himself. He was quiet but, thought Gina, rather sullen. She resolved to try to talk to him after class.

Near the end of the class, Gina drew the students' attention to the side board where the anthem was written. "Mrs. Menor has asked us all to go over this anthem before Friday, because we'll be singing it at the assembly. Let's run through the words together." While the students recited, Russell stood up and started moving toward the door. "Russell, sit down," said Gina sternly. He countered, "It's lunchtime. I'm just going to lunch." Without Gina leading, the class faltered in their reciting and stopped, eagerly listening—as high school students always do—to a potential conflict. "We're not done here yet," Gina reminded him. Russell looked straight at her and said, in a calm voice, "Look, to be real honest, Ms. Harris, I just don't see no point in staying around for some white teacher to teach me a black song."

QUESTIONS TO CONSIDER

1. What was the purpose of presenting this poem at the assembly?
2. What is your reaction to the poem? What would your reaction be as an African-American student in the assembly? as a white student? an Asian student?
3. Is this poem appropriate for the assembly? Is it appropriately presented?
4. With which student teacher's ideas do you identify, if any? With whom do you disagree and why?
5. Was there any attempt at multicultural education in your own middle and high school years? Do you think the needs of all the students in your school were met?

6. Is it possible for white teachers to teach black history and culture effectively? Is it legitimate for them to teach it?

7. Why do you think Gina feels uncomfortable talking to James about her questions?

8. How would you suggest that Gina broach the subject?

9. What do you know about the Black National Anthem?

10. How do Gina's questions appear from James's point of view?

11. How do you think Gina should plan to present the Black National Anthem to her students?

12. Why do you think Russell challenged Gina in this way? What is he thinking?

13. How should Gina respond to Russell?

14. What might she have done differently to avoid this conflict?

RECOMMENDED READINGS

Banks, J. A. (1988). *Multiethnic education theory and practice,* (2nd ed.). Boston: Allyn & Bacon.

    This textbook for teacher education includes sections on the history, goals, and practices in multiethnic education; the ideological and philosophical issues; and the problems which its implementation presents. The final section suggests teaching strategies for the classroom.

Crichlow, W., Goodwin, S., Shakes, G., & Swartz, E. (1990). Multicultural ways of knowing. *Journal of Education,* 172(2), 101–117.

    The authors describe the evolution of multicultural education in the United States as a traditional struggle over the content of curriculum. They suggest that today this struggle is over much more than the quantifiable representations of minority groups.

Duchene, M. (1988). GIANT LAW, GIANT EDUCATION, and ANT: A story about racism and Native Americans. *Harvard Education Review,* 58(3), 354–362.

    The author gives a brief overview of the history of racist oppression of Native Americans. She further explains that in their oral tradition, Native Americans have relied heavily on metaphors and analogies to relate their experience of racism. Ms. Duchene relates one such story which she says could be told about racism in education and law. ANT, GIANT LAW, and GIANT EDUCATION are the symbolic protagonists.

Lee, C., et al. (1990). How shall we sing our sacred song in a strange land? *Journal of Education,* 172(2), 45–61.

    The authors present an explanation of the need for an African-centered pedagogy for African-American students, examine the problems inherent in its development, focusing on how it fits into a multiethnic society, and suggest a set of goals for an effective African-centered education.

Paley, V. (1979). *White Teacher.* Boston: Harvard University Press.

The author recounts her experience teaching in an ethnically mixed kindergarten. This book could serve as an effective starting point for discussion about teacher education students' own feelings regarding subtle racism and prejudice.

Parkay, F. W. (1983). *White Teacher, Black School: The Professional Growth of a Ghetto Teacher.* New York: Praeger.

This book is an account of the experiences and analyses of another white teacher in a black school. Parkay relates examples of hope and despair and his reflections on these experiences. He finishes with some suggestions for how we must change to be more effective educators in the inner-city classroom.

Saunders, M. (1982). *Multicultural teaching: A guide for the classroom.* London: McGraw-Hill.

Saunders's purpose is twofold: to sensitize teachers to the existence of and effects of racism in education and to help teachers develop the knowledge base to evaluate, develop, and teach multicultural curricula. Each chapter examines a different question which concerned educators commonly ask.

Schniedewind, N., & Davidson, E. (1983). *Open minds to equality: A sourcebook of learning activities to promote race, sex, class, and age equity.* Englewood Cliffs, NJ: Prentice-Hall.

This book is a collection of detailed learning activities designed to help students explore their ideas of what is and is not fair in our society, and to help develop effective strategies to combat inequality. Topics addressed include gender, race, class, and age equity.

Schofield, J. (1989). *Black and White Together in School: Trust, Tension, or Tolerance?* New York: Teacher's College Press.

This book reports the results of a three-year longitudinal ethnographic study of a recently desegregated middle school. Through observations and interviews, the author examined the reactions of administrators, students, and teachers to the new environment.

Sleeter, C. E., & Grant, C. A. (1988). *Making choices for multicultural education: Five approaches to race, class and gender.* Columbus, OH: Merrill.

This book addresses not only issues of race and culture, but also gender, language, social class, and disability. The authors identified five different approaches to multicultural education, and this book includes a chapter on each, concluding with the authors, argument for their preferred approach: education that is multicultural and social reconstructionist.

THE ADVISER/ADVISEE PROBLEM

ALLAN A. GLATTHORN

ABSTRACT

Bob Grunewald is a new teacher assigned to the middle school in the Warren School District. The district serves a community that had once been an all-white middle-class enclave but has recently become more diverse in its ethnic makeup. Bob is very interested in multicultural education but seems given to stereotyping minorities. The principal, Gene Stillman, often seems to project a condescending attitude and is most concerned about keeping matters under control.

Bob institutes the use of dialogue journals in his adviser group, telling the students that they can write anything they want. Three journal entries cause him concern. Walter Jackson, an African-American, complains that Bob's emphasis on African-American culture embarrasses him. Gail Swanson, a white girl, writes that her parents object strongly to her affection for Walter Jackson and that she is considering suicide. Loc, a Vietnamese student, is often moody and withdrawn, leading Bob to suspect that he is the victim of child abuse.

Bob's problems come to a head in his first meeting with the principal. Stillman suggests that Bob decrease his use of small groups, that he abandon his dialogue journals, and that he deemphasize the multicultural aspects of his classes. He suggests that Bob emphasize similarities, not differences.

The Adviser/Advisee Problem

Bob Grunewald had just joined the faculty of the Warren Middle School as a social studies/language arts teacher assigned to the eighth grade. Bob was a recent graduate of Central State, which has a strong middle school program; he looked forward eagerly to his assignment. He had developed a special interest in adviser/advisee programs and hoped at some point to become a counselor. His own years as a middle school student had not been happy ones. He had been a shy young teenager with few friends, and he had determined that he would help middle school students have a happier school life than he had had.

The Warren School District was a medium-sized suburban school system bordering a large city and serving chiefly a lower- to middle-class community. Years ago it had been an all-white middle-class enclave, with a reputation for excellence. The community had undergone some major changes, however. More affluent families had fled farther to the exurbs, and upwardly mobile working-class families had replaced them, fleeing the adjoining city. For years there had been subtle attempts on the part of real estate agents and township officials to keep the district white, but both legal and financial pressures had made that goal impossible. Racism seemed to persist among many of the white families that made up the majority. At the time Bob joined the Warren faculty, the demographic data showed this mix in the student body: White, 68 percent; African-American, 14 percent; Hispanic-American, 10 percent; Asian-American, 8 percent.

Bob participated in the pre-school orientation sessions for new teachers. The superintendent began with a lengthy address in which she extolled the virtues of the Warren schools, giving special attention to the district's new initiative in "Total Quality Management," assuring all the new teachers that they would play a vital role in this new initiative. The assistant superintendent for instruction followed the superintendent. He also praised the school district, focusing on the district's recent decision to use an Outcomes-Based Education model in improving student achievement. He summarized his remarks with the following comments. "You'll be involved in many workshops to give you the skills you need to make your teaching outcomes-based. Just remember, to implement the curriculum, plan units so that they relate to our outcomes, and teach lessons so that they relate to the units. It's as simple as that."

All the new teachers then returned to the schools to which they had been assigned, to meet with the principal for school-based orientation. At the meeting at Warren Middle, Bob was joined by three other new teachers—Ed Jordan, a young African-American who also would teach social studies and language arts; Jack Tomlinson, recently discharged from the military, assigned to teach science and mathematics; and Holly Watkins, a young woman who would be teaching health and physical education.

The principal, Gene Stillman, began with a brief welcome, telling the four new teachers that they had joined an excellent faculty of professionals who had successfully initiated the "middle school concept" just three years ago. He noted that the only area where they had not met with complete success was with the adviser/advisee program.

"Frankly, some of our teachers are a little afraid of the adviser/advisee program, I think, because they fear that they have to function as guidance counselors. I have explained to them that it really exists as an extended adviser period, which gives them some time to build group coherence. And that's my advice to you new people. There are many activities that you can get your group involved in, such as decorating one of our big bulletin boards or making a float for the high school homecoming parade. Just don't let it become a homework period. There is already too much of that going on. I know from our interview, Bob, that you have a special interest in the adviser-advisee program; I hope you can give us some help here."

Stillman then talked more about the school's programs and student body. "We have a very strong gifted program. And I might note that we have some really outstanding Asian students who are part of that. Last year there were two Black students in the gifted program—youngsters from very fine families. I know that your professors talked about the research on ability grouping, and I know they all recommend heterogeneous grouping. But we still see a need to separate our gifted youngsters for some accelerated work. At the other end, we have just developed a *Challenge* program for the poor project kids."

Bob asked, "Who are the project kids?"

Stillman smiled apologetically. "I'm sorry; I should have explained. We have on the edge of our township a housing project for poor folk. They're mostly Black and Hispanic families. They're good people now, but they just don't give the school much support. We work hard at involving them in the parent organization, but with no luck. And we know that those projects are not a good learning environment. So this *Challenge* program will have the youngsters and their parents come to the school on Saturday morning for some intensive work on the computers to improve their reading and math abilities. We're going to announce the new program a few weeks after school starts. We'll have the district social worker and our guidance counselor help us identify the at-risk youngsters. We'll then send notices home to the parents, inviting them to take part in this new program."

The last part of the day was devoted to a meeting with the mentors who had been assigned to the new teachers. Bob's mentor was Roger Marcus, a veteran eighth-grade science teacher. Roger was direct and to the point. "The main thing is to start out tough. Spend the first few days drilling your students with the routines you plan to use. Start the first day with some solid content; that will give them a signal that you mean business. If you need any help, give me a call."

Bob thanked Roger for his advice. Roger continued, "I heard Gene Stillman say you had some interest in the adviser-advisee program. Let me be honest with you. Stillman's a good principal, but he doesn't know how tough this adviser program is. But I finally got it licked. I have developed for each adviser meeting a game we play, such as a word game or a trivia contest. I divide the kids into teams. At the end of each marking period we see which team won. The winning team gets some ice cream. Why don't you try my games? It'll make things a whole lot easier for you."

Bob respectfully declined. "Thanks a lot. But I really would like to try my own approach."

Roger seemed slightly offended. "Suit yourself."

First-Week Difficulties

Bob struggled through the first four days of classes, experiencing some serious problems with classroom discipline. He tried to be friendly with the students; they took advantage of his friendliness. He then tried getting tough but had trouble following through on his threats. He looked forward eagerly to the first meeting of his adviser group on Friday; he had been assigned twenty youngsters whom he also taught for English and social studies.

On Friday morning he greeted his advisees enthusiastically. Their ethnic diversity corresponded approximately to the school's: 13 White students; 3 African-American; 3 Hispanic-American; 1 Asian-American. After telling them something about himself and having them introduce themselves, he explained what his adviser group would be doing.

"One of the most interesting things that you'll be doing is keeping a dialogue journal. Your dialogue journal is your chance to get things off your chest. You can write about anything you want—your classes, your hopes, your fears, your family, your friends. And you write just on the right-hand side of your journal. That leaves me the left-hand side to respond to what you have written. That's why we call it a dialogue journal: you and I have some dialogue. We'll take part of each adviser period to do some journal writing, but you also will be expected to write on your own outside of class."

Bob was disappointed that the class did not seem enthusiastic about the idea, but he pressed ahead.

"So let's get started. I'm passing out some guidelines for the dialogue journal and a brown copybook you can use. Any questions?"

Walter Jackson, a tall African-American boy, said, "I don't know why we have to write in journals. Can't we just talk and not write all the time?"

"I understand your feelings, Walter. I know that in the Black culture, oral communication is preferred to written. I just want you to give it a try for the first marking period. Then we all will take a good look at how it has worked." Walter seemed annoyed but said nothing.

Bob continued. "You have your journal book and the guidelines. I want you all to write about this question: 'Should parents have the right to dictate the kinds of friends you have?' My parents really controlled me; they wanted me to pick friends who were from my own social class. And I know that it must be an important issue for all of you. There are no easy answers. You write what you think about that. Then we'll talk in small groups about your answers."

Dialogue Journal Guidelines

1. Write in your journal anything you want to write. Use the right-hand page only.
2. If you don't want me to read what you have written, fold the page in half and staple it closed. I promise not to peek.
3. Please feel free to let me know what you think about our class and our adviser group. But if you want to criticize some other teacher, use a name like *Mr. X* or *Ms. Y*.
4. I will collect the journals every Friday and return them to you by Monday. You must have three journal entries for each week.
5. I will give you a grade for your journals at the end of the marking period; you will be judged just on how much you write and how honest you are. I will not take off for spelling, punctuation, or grammar.

REMEMBER THAT THE JOURNAL IS YOUR CHANCE TO EXPRESS YOUR FEELINGS AND TO COMMUNICATE HONESTLY WITH ME.

The students opened their journals to a blank page, but it was obvious to Bob that most of them were not excited by the opportunity. He let them work on their own for a few minutes before monitoring their work. As he walked around the room, he noticed that most of them had written only one or two sentences. He noted only two exceptions to this general pattern. Gail Swanson, daughter of a school board member, was writing furiously. After ten minutes of writing, she seemed to have filled several pages.

And Loc, a Vietnamese boy, seemed to spend the entire time staring off into space. He had not written a word. Bob stopped by his desk and patted him on the shoulder. "Don't think, Loc; just write. Just let the words flow." Loc seemed to withdraw from his touch and smiled weakly, nodding his head. Bob made a mental note to keep a close eye on Loc. Maybe they should talk after school one day.

Bob called a halt after fifteen minutes. "OK, you had a chance to organize your thinking. Now it's time to talk. I'm going to call your names and give you your group number. Each group will have about five members. Choose a leader and a recorder. Discuss your ideas openly. Then we'll see what you all think."

He called their names and their numbers and assigned each an area of the room where they could meet. It seemed to take them a long time just to get settled, and their talking seemed really noisy. In the midst of this commotion, the principal arrived. He stood at the door for a few minutes, stopped by two groups to observe briefly, and then exited. Bob sensed he was displeased. He didn't know whether he should see Stillman that afternoon to explain what the class was doing or wait to see if the principal called him in for a conference.

Bob then looked at the clock with dismay. Only three minutes were left. "We'll have to stop this now and pick it up next Friday."

Angelo said, "We were just picking a recorder. There was no time to talk."

"I know. We'll have more time next week. Remember to keep your journals. I'll collect them at the end of the period next Friday."

As Walter was leaving the classroom, Bob detained him briefly. He wanted to be sure there was no misunderstanding or bad feeling. "I appreciated your very honest question, Walter. I'm glad you're part of this adviser group." Walter seemed uninterested in talking and began to turn toward the door. Bob made one more attempt to show that he meant well. "Are you on the school's basketball team, Walt?"

Walter reacted with what seemed to be sullen rejection. "I don't play basketball. And I don't like jazz." He walked away. Bob was puzzled by his response.

The second week passed with some slight improvement in discipline. He and the students seemed to have worked out an unspoken truce: they would not misbehave as long as he was not too demanding. Gradually he was achieving enough control so that the class settled down after ten minutes of chatter. Bob felt that he had to be flexible about starting class, since the students had an obvious need to talk with their friends.

Bob especially enjoyed the social studies class. He explained to them that it would not be a standard "White man's view" of American history, but would give special attention to the contributions of minorities, especially "Blacks," as he called them.

The second session of the adviser group also seemed to go a bit better. Bob took the first fifteen minutes of the period to let them talk in groups about parent control of friendship. Then each group reported briefly. All the groups reported strong opposition to any parent control and most spoke about their resentment of parent influence. Bob took a neutral stance. "You have to keep thinking about it and talking it over with your parents."

Then for the last part of the period he had them write in their journals on a new topic. "The issue for this week is corporal punishment. That means physically punishing someone. I want you to write about it from both a school and home perspective. Do you think that schools should ever use corporal punishment? Do you think parents should use corporal punishment? You can write for the rest of this period. Then we'll have the group discussions next Friday."

Bob eagerly anticipated reading the journals he collected at the end of class Friday. Saturday morning he sat at the kitchen table and began to read. Most had only very brief entries, indicating strong opposition to parent influence. Two entries caught his attention. On one page, Walter Jackson had written this in large letters: PLEASE GET OFF THE SUBJECT OF AFRICAN-AMERICANS.

Bob was really disturbed. He had hoped that Walter would feel especially interested in a multicultural approach to history, and he was puzzled by the reaction. He wrote on the facing page, "Sorry I upset you. Let's talk."

The second entry that bothered him was Gail's. She had written a long and anguished statement about her strong affection for Walter and her parents' vehement opposition. It seemed to Bob like a desperate cry for help. He wrote on the facing page, "I understand your feelings. Let's talk."

That week he made a special point of asking both Walter and Gail to see him after school. Walter came reluctantly. "I was disturbed by your journal entry, Walter. What did I do that upset you?"

Walter stared at him for a long time before answering. "My father's a doctor. My mother's a teacher. I want to get a good education. I know all about the African-American culture."

Bob responded, "You're right, of course. But I think the rest have to be educated."

Walter stared at him, seemingly unconvinced. "The more you and the other teachers talk, the more the other guys resent me."

Bob said, "You've given me a lot to think about. Let's keep our communication open, OK?" Walter shrugged noncommittally and left the room.

The conference with Gail was even more upsetting. Gail began crying almost at once. She talked about her deep love for Walter, painting her parents as tyrants and racists. "I feel I can really talk to you, Mr. Grunewald. You really seem to understand kids. My parents are really old. They've lost touch. I really feel hopeless. Some days it doesn't seem worth going on. Do you think that maybe you and I could talk like this a couple of times a week?"

Bob felt flattered but also a bit awkward. "I'm not a counselor, Gail. You ought to talk with Miss Armstrong, the counselor."

"I've tried and it does no good. She is always looking at her watch and thinking of her next appointment. She tells me just to obey my parents."

"Well, I don't want to listen to you criticize her. That would be unprofessional. But if you think I can help, why not stop by tomorrow after school?"

That afternoon he decided to stop in to see Armstrong. "I'm concerned about Gail Swanson, Miss Armstrong. She really seems almost suicidal. What can you tell me about her?"

Armstrong smiled cynically. "So she's gotten to you, has she? She pulls that act on every new teacher. She flirts with all these black kids, since no white kid will look at her. Sure her parents are upset. They suspect she's having intercourse with that Jackson kid. Wouldn't you be upset? The best thing to do is just ignore her."

Bob wasn't fully convinced. "You know her better than I, of course. And I'm no expert. It's just that I thought I picked up some suicidal tendencies."

Armstrong patted him on the shoulder. "I'm glad you came to see me. And I appreciate your concern. If I tried to fix up every moody mixed-up fourteen-year-old girl, I'd be running a psychiatric ward, not a guidance office. I'll have her in for a talk, though, as soon as all these schedule changes get made. I know we can't ignore these things."

Bob was still gravely concerned. He just didn't know what else he should do.

The third adviser session began with the group discussion of corporal punishment. Bob let the discussion run for fifteen minutes. Then he started the group reports. All the groups except one seemed unanimous in condemning corporal punishment. Ashley said to the class, "We had some really good discussion in our group. Most of us were opposed to corporal punishment, but Loc told us that in the Vietnamese culture, parents are expected to use corporal punishment with their children." Several members of the class gasped in surprise. Loc seemed deeply embarrassed.

Bob said, "Loc, could you tell us more about that?" Loc shook his head "no" and stared down at his desk. Bob tried to ease the embarrassment. "See, that's the point, class. Every culture is different."

As the class left, Bob felt torn by what had been said about Vietnamese parents. Then he thought about some troubling signs he had noted in observing Loc closely for the first few weeks. One morning he had come in with a large lump over his eye, explaining to Bob that a baseball had hit him. And he always seemed moody and depressed. Maybe Loc was being abused. Bob had heard all about the law on reporting child abuse and knew he had a responsibility.

Except for these individual problems, Bob felt that in general things were going well. His classes seemed at least to be tolerating him. And the adviser group finally seemed to be understanding and profiting from the journal-discussion format. He was feeling rather positive then, when he was asked to report for his first conference with Gene Stillman.

The Principal's Ultimata

Stillman opened the conference by asking Bob how things were going. Bob replied with enthusiasm. "My classes are really going well. We do a lot of small group work, and the students seem to like it. I am trying to integrate language arts and social studies, and the other teachers have been a big help. And the adviser groups are working fine."

Stillman answered, "Well, you touched on two matters that are of concern—your use of small groups and your use of those journals. First, with the small groups. That first day I stopped in, the groups really seemed confused and off-task. I like cooperative learning, but I think you're rushing it too much. My advice to you is that you hold off using any more small groups until you have full control and until you have taught those youngsters how to operate in groups."

Bob was discomfited but felt he had to seem agreeable. "That's a good suggestion, Mr. Stillman. I'll try that approach."

"Good," Stillman replied. "Now the journal is the more serious problem. I've received several complaints from the parents about those journals. They feel that you're meddling and turning their children against them."

Bob was aghast. "I don't meddle. I don't choose sides. I just want to give the students a chance to express their feelings. Which parents are complaining?"

Stillman answered in what seemed to be a patronizing tone. "Bob, I can't tell you which parents; I promised them confidentiality. And that's not the issue. Let me help you understand my concern. You're a new teacher here; I've been in this community for twenty years. We're working with a very conservative community. They don't want the schools talking about values. They feel that that's a family concern. I don't always agree, but you can't have a good school without parent support. And, from my perspective, teachers can't be neutral about supporting the parents. You have to choose sides. We're on the side of the parents. Look, why don't I meet with all you new teachers and clarify this question for all of you? I know that you weren't intentionally causing trouble, and I don't want it to be a problem between you and me."

Bob felt himself torn. He was convinced that Stillman was wrong, but he didn't want to challenge him directly.

"Well, Mr. Stillman, I appreciate your calling these matters to my attention. I'll have to give them some thought."

"Well, Bob, there is no need for thought. I think you had better end the journal keeping—at least until the second term. That will give us some time to work out this problem. I've also asked Mr. Marcus to work with you. He's your mentor. And he does an excellent job with the adviser group. I want you to talk with him tomorrow at the latest."

Bob decided not to object, although he was seething inside. He started to get up.

"Wait, Bob. There is one more somewhat delicate matter. Some of your youngsters have been complaining to their parents that you talk too much about cultural differences. Let me help you understand what our goals are here. First, I want to create in this school a sense of community where we emphasize how we are similar, not how we are different. And I told you that we're working with a very conservative community. The parents want us to emphasize traditions we have in common. Now we have revised our U. S. history course to give due attention to minorities. But I don't think it's wise to talk too much about cultural differences."

Bob felt he had to disagree. "With all due respect, Mr. Stillman, I think we have to talk about differences. The school has a mixed population. They should be proud of their differences."

"Bob, don't mix up our long-term goal with our short-term strategy. At some point in the future, this community will be ready to talk about cultural differences and see them as strengths. That's an ideal I believe in. But they're not ready for that. This community is a good place for Blacks and Hispanics and Asians. When those riots in Los Angeles occurred, this town was quiet. And you don't hear people talking about the things that divide us.

"You don't know this, of course, but we've had some good discussions in our parents' group about the pros and cons of multicultural education. We all agreed that the school should take a middle-of-the-road course: teach the contributions of minorities, but emphasize the Western tradition. And the parents made it very clear that they did not want teachers talking about controversies that involve the minorities. Our short-term strategy in the school, therefore, is to talk about the things that unite us—to keep building school spirit.

"You and I can have our private differences about that. And I'm not telling you to ignore the contributions of Blacks. I was one of the first in this town to support making King's birthday a holiday. I just want you to know that your own students are feeling uncomfortable with all the talk about their cultural differences. And I'm just suggesting for your own good that you not talk so much in class about the minority groups who are sitting in front of you." Stillman closed by putting his arm around Bob's shoulder as they walked toward the office door. "You're doing a good job as a new teacher, Bob. I just think you have to keep in mind the things we talked about. And we all want to help you make this first year a successful one."

QUESTIONS TO CONSIDER

1. How effective was the orientation for new teachers? If you were planning the program for the first day of orientation, how would you change it?

2. How would you characterize the attitudes of the principal, Gene Stillman, toward the African-American students? What evidence can you provide?

3. How successful do you think the *Challenge* program will be? What reasons can you advance for your prediction?

4. Do you think that Bob was wise in rejecting Roger's offer of help? What are the reasons for your opinion?

5. Do you think Bob was wise in using dialogue journals at the start of the year? Explain your position.

6. Do you believe that Bob's response to Walter (about the preferred communication style of African-Americans) was appropriate? Why or why not?

7. Do you think Bob's choice of topic for the first use in the dialogue journal was appropriate? Explain your position.

8. In what ways could Bob have made this first session with his adviser group more effective?

9. If you were Bob, would you have initiated a conference with the principal to explain the commotion that the principal observed?

10. How do you explain Walter's comment: "I don't play basketball. And I don't like jazz."

11. Was Bob wise in taking a neutral stance about the issue of parental influence on children's friendships?

12. Was Bob's second choice of topic for the journal writing a good one?

13. Walter uses the term *African-American* to identify his ethnic group. Bob, the teachers, and the principal use the term *Black*. Does the term make any difference? Which term do you think the educators should use?

14. What do you think Bob should do in response to Walter's request that he "get off the subject of African-Americans"?

15. What do you think Bob should do about his concern for Gail's emotional health?

16. What do you think Bob should do about his suspicion that Loc is being abused?

17. Do think Stillman's advice to defer small group work is sound? If you were Bob, how would you have responded to Stillman?

18. If you were Bob, how would you have responded in that office conference to Stillman's order to discontinue the journal writing until the second term? Would you implement his order if further discussion proved futile?

19. Do you think Stillman is wise in his advice about minimizing the discussion of cultural differences? If you were Bob, would you take his advice?

20. What should the district leaders, the school principal, and the mentor have done to make Bob's first few weeks more successful?

21. In what ways did Bob contribute to his own problems? How would you characterize Bob's attitudes toward minorities?

22. To what extent should the school district's multicultural education policies and practices be determined by the views of the community?

RECOMMENDED READINGS

Banks, J. A. (1991). *Teaching strategies for ethnic studies,* (5th ed.). Boston: Allyn & Bacon.

    Considered one of the basic sources in multicultural education.

Casanova, U. (1987). Ethnic and cultural differences. In V. Richardson-Koehler (ed.), *Educator's handbook: A research perspective*. New York: Longman.

    Summarizes in a useful manner the research on the issue of cultural differences and their implications for the classroom.

George, P. S., & Alexander, W. M. (1992). *Exemplary middle schools,* (2d ed.). Orlando, FL: Harcourt Brace.

　　One of the best overall sources on middle school issues; includes a very helpful discussion of adviser-advisee programs.

James, M. (1986). *Adviser-advisee programs: Why, what, and how.* Columbus, OH: National Middle Schools Association.

　　An excellent "how-to" manual on such programs.

Ogbu, J. G. (1992, November). Understanding cultural diversity and learning. *Educational Researcher, 21* (8), 5–14.

　　An excellent article that reviews approaches to multicultural education and presents a research-based understanding of why certain minorities experience difficulty in school.

Ravitch, D. (1991, December). A culture in common. *Educational Leadership, 49* (4), 8–11.

　　Argues for the need to emphasize our shared traditions, not cultural differences.

Sergiovanni, T. J. (1992). *Moral leadership: Getting to the heart of school improvement.* San Francisco: Jossey-Bass.

　　Presents a persuasive rationale for moral leadership that transcends parochial issues.

Zanger, V. V. (ed.). (1990). *Drawing on diversity.* Boston: Boston Public Schools.

　　A useful resource for multicultural education; includes materials written by Vietnamese on the use of corporal punishment in raising children.

BRAD HILL: THE ONE AND ONLY

BETTY A. HALLENBECK

ABSTRACT

Brad Hill is a 175-pound sixth grader who is nearly six feet tall. He is the only African-American in the small town of Taylor and is often ridiculed for being different. In school, at home, and in the community Brad's behavior is often violent and noncompliant. After six years of refusing to allow Brad to be evaluated for special education placement, Brad's mother has finally signed the consent form. Now the problem is getting the psychologists to actually do the testing. In the meantime, Brad's teacher and principal struggle to manage his behavior at school. The special education teacher, who has served Brad illegally for several months now, is especially frustrated because she realizes that even if Brad qualifies for special services, the school district does not have a placement which meets his needs. This is a case of a student who falls through the cracks, agencies that do not work together, and a school district that violates most procedural guidelines for delivering special services.

Brad Hill: The One and Only

Moment of Truth

Brad's eyes shine with pure hatred. He clenches his teeth, raises his fist slightly higher, and trembles uncontrollably. Anger engulfs him, drowning out reason and obliterating his sense of control.

In the 8 months that I have known him, I have never seen Brad like this. Standing before him, my mind quickly scrolls through potential responses. When I realize that we are completely alone in the school, panic washes over me. After 5 years as a special education teacher I am adept at interpreting the nuances of children's behavior. I know how serious this is. At 5 feet 11 inches tall, this sixth grader outweighs me by more than 65 pounds. He is powerful already, and I know that children in the throes of rage often display unusual strength.

Instinctively, I begin talking to Brad. Years of practice allow me to speak calmly and gently, not betraying my own fear. "It's OK, Brad. It's fine to be angry," I hear myself say, as if from a great distance. "Remember on Friday how angry you were? We got through that really well. It's OK to be angry, but I can't help you if you hurt me." I keep on this way, softly speaking to him, avoiding any eye contact, for several minutes. This approach has quieted him in the past, and it is all I have to go with now.

At first, he does not respond. Then, abruptly, he grabs a textbook and slams it onto a desk. "Shut up, bitch. I don't need any help from your white ass." His voice has a caustic edge to it which reveals rising fury.

I have to do something. "Brad, I know you're very angry. You know that I want to help you. Since my talking is making you madder, I'm going to be quiet now so that you can think clearly and make the best choice about what to do. I know you will make the right choice."

I take a slow, deep breath and force myself to relax. Standing very still, I wait and think about how all of this has come to pass.

A Bit of Background

Although Brad spent at least half of each day in my classroom, he was not yet identified as a special education student. He was allowed to be in my special education class through a procedure called diagnostic placement. This loophole, which I knew to be patently illegal, was intended to allow short-term placement of students in the Educational

Resource Center (ERC) when a standard evaluation was considered inadequate. Brad had been referred for a complete evaluation more than 5 months ago, and we still had not held an eligibility meeting. I had completed the academic portion of his testing within a week after we received parental permission to test. The psychologists, however, had not yet begun their work with him. I was furious. Brad needed intensive services, and he needed them now.

Brad was the only person of African-American heritage in all of Taylor, a town of about 7,000 people on the east side of the Cascade Range in the Pacific Northwest. With the exception of the occasional migrant worker, he was the only non-Caucasian in town. He lived with his mother, Roxie, who was white, and his half-brother in a small home close to Ponderosa School. His mother's boyfriend moved in and out of the house as did a cast of other characters from all over the state.

I have visited Brad's home many times, although I no longer will go there without at least one other person. His mother, and any other adults who happen to be there, openly drink and use drugs as we discuss ways to help Brad. The air in the house is oppressive. Radiators pump out stifling heat; smoke obscures furniture just a few feet away. There are cats everywhere; the smell of their urine permeates everything. People emerge from nowhere, sometimes mumbling or moaning, other times yelling obscenities at each other. At home, Brad is nearly invisible. He is camouflaged by the chaos of his surroundings. He sits subdued and obedient, a totally different child from the one I see in school.

I was staggered by Brad's school history. I still find myself reexamining his records, unable to believe that I've understood them correctly. Since kindergarten, Brad had missed 290 days of school. He was always in trouble when he did attend school, and notes in his file indicated that his absences were viewed as blessings. Suspension accounted for more than 25 percent of his absences. Because he had missed so much school, his skill acquisition had been extremely irregular. He had a history of defiance, aggression, truancy, and poor work habits that went back to kindergarten. Before this year, teachers and administrators simply ignored his absences. Despite his slightly above average ability level, Brad was at least 3 years below grade level in all academic areas.

Brad, In Person

I noticed Brad immediately on the first day of classes. He towered above the other students and most of the teachers. He seemed to revel in the advantages his size afforded him, intimidating others whenever opportunities presented themselves. If his size had not drawn people's attention to Brad, his dark skin and curly hair would have. In this conservative ranching community, Brad's presence was an aberration. Most people here did not accept Brad. The other children feared him. They could not ignore his size, his reputation, or his uniqueness.

Shortly after school started, Lucille, the principal, asked me if we could discuss Brad at our first School Wide Assistance Team (SWAT) meeting. I had been in too many schools where these teams served as "get this kid out of my room" groups and vowed to run this one differently. I envisioned a supportive place where teachers could discuss their problems and triumphs with each other. I was committed to this process and worked hard to make it a success. Brad would test my ability to keep the tone of these meetings professional and solution-oriented.

The day before our SWAT meeting, Lucille called me into her office to fill me in on Brad's history. She had known him since kindergarten, although he had not always attended her school. In fact, in the past 6 years Brad had been enrolled in each of the 6 elementary schools in our district for varying amounts of time. This was the result of Roxie's attempts to find a school which understood Brad and could manage his behavior. When Brad's behavior began to cause problems in one school, Roxie would simply transfer him to a different building. Tired of working with Roxie and investing time in Brad, administrators allowed these transfers. Brad had come full circle and was enrolled once again in the school where he had gone to kindergarten.

Lucille believed that Roxie was the cause of most of Brad's problems. She thought that Roxie felt intensely guilty about her affair with an African-American man which had produced Brad. Roxie refused to reprimand Brad for his behavior, no matter how violent or disrespectful. She vehemently defended his every action and actually instructed him to "beat the crap out of people" whenever he needed to. On one occasion, Brad had lost the opportunity to go on a field trip by violating the terms of a contract written to help him earn that privilege. Roxie, who had agreed to the contract, had to be removed from the school by the police. She threatened the principal by saying, "I'll mop this office with your head, you fucking bitch," and blocking Lucille's exit from the room.

Listening to all of this, I started to realize the severity of Brad's problems. I left Lucille's office feeling discouraged and uneasy.

At our SWAT meeting, we devoted the entire 45 minutes to Brad. Every adult in the school who would have contact with him was present. Many of them wanted to take this time to complain about Brad's past, offer gloomy predictions for his future, and lament their own misfortune at having to teach this boy. I struggled to keep the group focused, to redirect them so that we could help Brad have a better year. Eventually we agreed on a plan for Brad: He would start the year with a clean slate. We would treat him like any other student, applying the consequences of our school's behavior management system as needed. We would not tolerate truancy or tardiness. We would contact Roxie frequently about his successes as well as his problems. We would expect Brad to be a successful, courteous student.

A New Plan for a New Year

For the first month or so, things went well for Brad. He was not a model student, but he seemed to be responding well to our consistent disciplinary system. Then things started to deteriorate. No single disastrous event heralded this change. Students were starting to complain that Brad had hurt or frightened them. Parents began sending notes or calling to express their concerns about Brad's behavior. His classroom teacher, Diane, reported that he was not completing assignments. Staff members described him as surly or mouthy. It was only October.

We spent another entire SWAT meeting talking about Brad. We did not want to suspend him unless it was necessary for his safety or the safety of others. This kid needed to be in school. We developed a new plan: Brad would be sent to my room when he needed a time-out. I would teach him a procedure for taking time out so that he wouldn't distract my other students. We all agreed to keep meticulous records of Brad's behavior. We would begin talking with Roxie, trying to persuade her to let us evaluate him. This seemed like a long shot, though, since Roxie had refused to give permission for Brad to be evaluated for each of the past 6 years.

While I was confident in my abilities to supervise Brad's time-outs, I had some reservations about our new plan. As is often the case in small school districts, my duties extended far beyond those usually assumed by a special education teacher. I already served 37 students with a wide range of disabilities. Some students came to the ERC for short periods of time each day. Others were with me for all of their academic classes. Several of my students had severe emotional and behavioral problems; one student was autistic, another trainably mentally retarded. Our district had no placement to meet their needs beyond the ERCs at each school.

To further complicate my job, our school was divided between two buildings which were located more than a block apart. With the help of 3 half-time assistants, I ran classrooms in both buildings simultaneously. As if this didn't keep me busy enough, I was also in charge of all new referrals for special services, triennial testing for my current students, and coordinating services with the Educational Service District (ESD) which provided psychological and related services. Finally, I served as acting principal whenever Lucille was unavailable. Since we had two campuses, this meant that I was in charge at least half of the time. Keeping track of Brad's time-outs was just one more thing to think about.

My assistants were very skeptical about having Brad in our room. Wendy and Tina, the two women who would work with him, were caring, conscientious people. Unfortunately, they had no training beyond what I had been able to provide. They were afraid of Brad. Nothing I could say seemed to reduce their apprehension. I worried that Brad would sense this and use it to his advantage.

Over the next month, I got to know Brad quite well. He had to take time-outs in my room several times a day. When this happened, my assistants were totally unable to work with him. He intimidated everybody, threw things, cursed, and made it impossible for instruction to continue. After Wendy came to me in tears and threatened to quit if she had to deal with Brad again, I realized that I personally would have to supervise his time-outs. If I was teaching in the primary building, this meant that I had to send my students back to their regular classes. Each time I had to send my eager second graders away from reading group to take care of Brad, I got angrier with him and with the school system.

Throughout these first months of school, Brad continued to miss school regularly. We documented these absences and eventually reported Roxie to the Assistant District Attorney. She was told that Brad must attend school regularly or she would be forced to pay a fine of $100 or serve jail time. Looking back at it now, our decision to do this marked the beginning of the end for Brad.

Roxie Pays a Visit

A few days after the District Attorney's office had delivered this news to Roxie, she paid us a visit at school. Lucille was out of town, and I was acting as principal. It was 8:45 a.m. and the hallway was crowded with children. The outside door near my classroom crashed open, and a husky voice yelled, "Where the hell is the goddamned principal?" When I stepped out of my classroom, Roxie spun on her heels, pointed my way, and bellowed, "Never mind. You'll do."

I knew that I had to get this woman away from the kids. Steeling myself for one of her antiauthority diatribes, I ushered Roxie into my classroom. As I closed the door, I sent one of my assistants to intercept the students who came to us at 9:00. They could work in the library while I conferred with Roxie. Knowing that Roxie had a reputation for creatively interpreting the truth to the superintendent and others in the central office, I sent for Julie, the school counselor, as a witness to our conversation.

Roxie refused to sit down, pacing the room instead and occasionally slamming her fist onto a desk. I watched her closely, trying to determine if she was on crack, if she was drunk, or if she was just furious. I tried to decide whether I should even attempt a conversation with her. Julie arrived, and we silently signaled each other that we would try to work through this.

After a brief silence, Roxie kicked a chair and exclaimed, "I'll make you pay for messing with my family, lady. You're a no-good bitch and that bastard principal is worse than you."

Modeling an approach I had seen Lucille use in these situations, I calmly answered her threats.

"Roxie, I want to work this out, but I will not stay here and listen to you threaten and insult me. If you do that again, I will leave." She hesitated for a moment, and then she sat down and began a familiar refrain.

"Braddy has gotten a bad deal from you people ever since he started school here. You don't understand him or what he's got to live with. People in this town spit on that kid. They hit him, scare him, and call him every name in the book. He may be big, but inside he's just a 12-year-old kid who don't deserve to be treated bad."

I had expected all of this.

Roxie was painfully accurate in her description of Brad's treatment by the locals. I had witnessed adults in town being cruel to Brad. No one deserved the humiliation that this boy had endured.

I tried to acknowledge Brad's tribulations while redirecting our conversation to the problem of his attendance. Roxie rejected each of my statements.

"I'm the kid's mother and there ain't nobody else who knows if he is OK to come to school. Some days I just got to keep him home. You people ain't got no right to choose if my boy comes to school."

We were at an impasse. Roxie didn't want to talk about Brad's school problems, and I refused to dwell on the home and community issues. Eventually Roxie decided to leave. Before she went, I managed to persuade her to agree to a complete evaluation of Brad. She was much calmer now, certain that the testing would support her interpretation of things, and even thanked me for taking time to talk with her. For the remainder of that day and over the long Thanksgiving weekend, I had an ominous feeling that this situation was about to deteriorate.

Brad Breaks the Law

On the first day back in school after the holiday, I was pulled out of class by an officer of the juvenile court. I didn't have to ask why. Over the vacation, Brad had apparently held a 10-inch butcher knife to the throat of an 8-year-old for nearly 20 minutes. He threatened to kill the girl because she was teasing him and people were being mean to him. Miraculously, a police officer had managed to dissuade Brad, and the girl had been unharmed.

The juvenile officer explained to me that Brad had been followed by the juvenile court for a long string of offenses starting at the age of 6. He had done $3,000 in damage to a church, destroyed other public property, shoplifted, loitered, and committed arson. In fourth grade, he had stolen the money earned by his classmates during a fund-raising event. He had also threatened and actually assaulted his own mother on several occasions. His sentences had always been lenient because of his age. This time, Brad would be forced to serve 100 hours of community service and to receive counseling. To me, these consequences were still too indulgent. I saw this incident as further evidence of Brad's need for intensive help. It frustrated and saddened me that the court system, as well as our own school district, seemed to ignore his needs.

In school that day, Brad reminded me of a caged animal. His extreme restlessness was punctuated by periods of complete inactivity. He was either agitated or in a stupor; there was no middle ground. Abandoning my other students to my assistants, I spent the entire day with Brad. Everything in his demeanor alarmed me. I resolved to light a fire under the psychologists at ESD. This child had to be evaluated as soon as possible. In the back of my mind, though, I wondered why I was bothering. No matter what they found, our district did not have a placement for Brad that would address his needs.

Within a matter of days, Brad became uncontrollable in the regular classroom. He did exactly what he wanted to do and seemed to delight in hurting other students. The kids in his class were terrified. Diane, one of the most experienced and talented teachers in our building, was discouraged and angry at herself. After an endless series of meetings, we settled on a diagnostic placement in my classroom. Until his testing was completed, Brad would spend from 8:45 until 12:00 each day with me. If he could not behave appropriately in the afternoon, Lucille and I would share responsibility for him.

My resentment of this whole situation was becoming tinged with hopelessness. I could not possibly do my job well under these conditions. I struggled to redefine my expectations and goals for the year. Brad required much more structure than I could possibly provide even if I stayed in one building all day. My other students were being woefully shortchanged, and I was asking the impossible of my assistants. Somewhat grudgingly, I vowed to make the best of this mess. After all, I was certain that within a few weeks Brad's testing would be done and we would officially discuss his eligibility and placement options.

Small Steps Forward

To my amazement, I actually enjoyed having Brad in my class. Faced with academic work which matched his skill level, Brad completed most of his assignments without complaint. He seemed to relish the fact that he was more advanced academically than other sixth graders who came to the ERC. With my guidance, he was able to help other students with their work and assume some responsibility in the classroom. For a time, he basked in his newly earned success. He became more amiable, and his aggressive behavior diminished markedly. I came to see a side of Brad which had previously been eclipsed by his aggressiveness and defiance. He was a talented artist with a flair for portraiture. He played the guitar and wrote poems. I was pleased that he chose to share his deeply personal creations with me and arranged for a local artist to work with him periodically. I took this as a sign that he was beginning to trust me and regained a bit of optimism about his situation.

More than three months passed this way. Brad was making steady progress academically, and his behavior was generally acceptable. He still had his days, though, when the slightest provocation would send him into a rage. And I still had to work with him personally. Leaving him alone with Wendy and Tina was an invitation to disaster.

Despite my weekly phone calls, strident letters, and personal visits to their supervisor, the psychologists who were to test Brad had barely started working with him. In their defense, they were given impossible caseloads, ridiculous time lines, and little support from our school district. Still, I learned from other special educators that students referred months later than Brad had already completed the eligibility process. I discovered that these psychologists had worked with Brad's older, seriously emotionally disturbed brother, Ted. One of the psychologists was scared of Brad and of his mother. These professionals were avoiding this case because of their own fears, and we were suffering because of it.

I was also discouraged because Brad was not going to counseling or serving his hours in the community as mandated by the court. To make matters worse, his juvenile officer conceded that there were no specific consequences for defying the edict of the court. Brad was learning that he could violate court orders without suffering any consequences. He was learning just how much he could get away with.

Small Steps Backward

In March, Brad started changing again in small but significant ways. He came to school exhausted, sometimes barely able to walk or speak sensibly. I began to wonder if he was drinking or using drugs. I asked him tentative questions about things at home, stressing that I was concerned for him and cared about his welfare. Some days he answered my questions in a sleepy, distant monotone. At other times, he would become infuriated that I dared intrude into his personal world. Patiently asking a question or two each morning, I eventually learned that his mother and her boyfriend were arguing violently and that the police had been called on many occasions. Also, his father had passed through town and had refused to see or speak to him. Finally, Ted was in serious legal trouble, and Brad feared that Ted would be removed from their home. I wasn't able to determine whether Brad was abusing any substances or simply suffering under the emotional strain of living in total chaos.

While he continued to behave well for me, Brad was causing more and more trouble around the school. He required Lucille or me to work with him at least 3 afternoons a week. In unstructured settings, like recess or walking down the hall, he often hit, kicked, or insulted other students. One day he held 3 terrified fourth graders hostage in the bathroom until their classroom teacher came looking for them. He had threatened them with very specific and painful forms of physical torture if they mentioned this to anybody. Brad was losing control, and I could do little for him beyond hoping that the psychologists would eventually do their job.

In the meantime, I researched private facilities in our region that worked with students like Brad. I doubted that our district would ever condone placing him in a residential school. Funding was so tight that last year we did not provide any busing for students. Still, I was determined to have as much information as I could in case we ever held that elusive placement meeting.

At about this time, a multiagency meeting was arranged to discuss Brad's situation. Lucille and I arrived at the meeting and saw 18 other people waiting to talk about this boy. Representatives of the juvenile court, children's services, the police department, the ESD, and two unfamiliar agencies described Brad's case. Each one of these people complained of feeling helpless. None of them would accept responsibility for doing anything that might help Brad. I cried as Lucille and I drove back to Taylor.

Brad Goes Too Far

We were in this precarious state, waiting for testing, trying to contain him, when Brad finally went too far. He maintained that another student had "looked at him funny" and so his behavior was justified. Walking up the ramp to his classroom, he jumped on this student's foot, twisted his arm behind his back, and threw him to the ground. I could see it all out my window and managed to sprint outside and yell his name just before Brad pounced on the child's back. Brad responded to me and stormed off without further injuring the other boy. It was this behavior that earned Brad an in-school suspension and cost him the opportunity to attend the special program with the rest of our students. This is how I came to be there, alone with him, grappling for ways to calm him down.

He had spent the entire day in my classroom and had behaved quite well. In fact, he seemed abnormally quiet and aloof. I interpreted this as fatigue or possibly sadness and didn't give it another thought. He was doing his work, my other students were getting the instruction they deserved, and the day was going smoothly. At 1:30 everybody in the building walked to a nearby school to attend a puppet show. Brad barely looked up as the other students filed past my room, chattering with excitement. At about 2:00 he began mumbling incoherently. Then he snapped. He flung his desk into the wall, breaking the top of it, and let out a horrifying wail. "I'm going to that damn show and you can't stop me!" he shouted. I leapt up and ran toward him as I began to explain why he must stay in my room. He placed himself in the center of the doorway, blocking my escape, and raised his fist just a few feet from my head.

As I wait for his choice and contemplate his story, my pity for Brad momentarily transcends my fear of him. I see him as the victim of a mismanaged, underfunded social service system. Out of fear or bias or carelessness, we have deserted this 12-year-old boy. I cannot fathom his anger and hatred, but I know that he is justified in whatever he feels. After another deep breath, I lift my eyes slightly, trying to decipher the level and direction of his wrath. It was a critical mistake to have allowed myself to be here alone with him, knowing him as I do. Let him make the choice, I think. Fear envelops me once more.

QUESTIONS TO CONSIDER

1. Why does the special education teacher choose to avoid eye contact and use a gentle voice in response to Brad's raised fist? What are potential advantages and disadvantages of this response to an aggressive student?

2. Explain how Brad came to be served in the special education class even though he had not yet been found eligible for special services. What procedure should have been followed before Brad was allowed to attend a special education class? Is it ever justifiable to circumvent established policies in this way?

3. To what extent did local residents' attitudes toward Brad contribute to his behavior problems?

4. How did Brad's home environment intensify his situation? Do you agree with the principal that Brad's mother was the main cause of his problems? Explain your answer.

5. Reconstruct Brad's school history from the information provided in this case. At what points could school officials have intervened to help Brad? Did the school district fulfill its responsibilities to Brad? Explain your answer.

6. Evaluate the responses of school personnel to Brad and Roxie throughout this case. In what ways did they react appropriately? What should they have done differently?

7. Explain Roxie's perspective of her son's situation. How should school personnel respond to Roxie's claims that they have caused Brad's behavior problems by misunderstanding him?

8. What is required in order for Brad to be successful in school? Can a public school design and implement a program to meet his needs? To what extent should the rights of other students be considered when deciding which educational placement is best for Brad?

9. The many agencies involved with Brad do not seem to be coordinating their efforts. Who is responsible for interagency communication? What steps can be taken to help agencies work together?

10. Describe the ways in which the system failed Brad. What could be done to increase the chances that students like Brad will get the services they need at an earlier age?

11. Throughout the case, Ellen, the special education teacher, is frustrated by her district's inability to meet Brad's needs and by the demands being placed on her. Where does a teacher's responsibility end in a case like this? What else could she do to help Brad get the services he requires?

RECOMMENDED READINGS

Algozzine, B., Ruhl, K., & Ramsey, R. (1991). *Behaviorally disordered? Assessment for identification and instruction.*
> This small book, part of the Council for Exceptional Children's mini-library on working with behavioral disorders, discusses all aspects of assessment of children with behavioral disorders.

Hallahan, D. P., & Kauffman, J. M. (1991). *Exceptional children: Introduction to special education.* Englewood Cliffs, NJ: Prentice-Hall, Simon & Schuster.
> This book would be most helpful for students wanting an overview of special education procedures and policies, such as the requirements of PL 94–142. Chapters 1, 5, and 11 are most relevant to this case.

Kauffman, J. M. (1993). *Characteristics of emotional and behavioral disorders of children and youth,* (5th ed.). New York: Merrill/Macmillan.
> Part 3 of this book (causal factors) and Chapter 12 (Conduct Disorder: Overt Aggression) are especially relevant to this case. These readings provide further information on the nature and causes of behavioral disorders.

Kerr, M. M., & Nelson, C. M. (1989). *Strategies for managing behavior problems in the classroom,* (2nd ed.). Columbus, OH: Merrill/Macmillan.
> This book is an excellent resource for students wanting to learn more about classroom management of behavior problems.

Nelson, C. M., & Pearson, C. A. (1991). *Integrating services for children and youth with emotional and behavioral disorders.* Reston, VA: Council for Exceptional Children.
> For students interested in interagency communication and provision of services for students with emotional and behavioral disorders, this book will be a valuable resource.

Wood, F., Cheney, C. O., Cline, D. H., Sampson, K., Smith, C. R., & Guetzloe, E. C. (1991). *Conduct disorders and social maladjustments: Policies, politics, and programming.* Reston, VA: Council for Exceptional Children.
> This small monograph includes discussion of many issues regarding service provision for students with conduct disorder.

"I DON'T KNOW. I JUST DON'T THINK YOU CAN BE A TEACHER."

CLAYTON KELLER, JOAN KARP, AND ELIZABETH QUINTERO

ABSTRACT

In this case, three student teachers—Connie, a white woman from a small, midwestern town; Lupe, an Hispanic-American from Texas; and Sarah, a woman with physical, communication, and learning disabilities—are teaching a lesson on discrimination to an eighth-grade class in American Studies. The lesson is observed by their university supervisor, Dr. Simon, who has called a meeting after school with some of the school staff to discuss whether Sarah should be a teacher. Lupe motivates the students to discuss their experiences with discrimination. Sarah starts slowly, but eventually engages the pupils in her lecture on discrimination legislation and litigation. Connie's discussion of To Kill a Mockingbird *fails. Dr. Simon praises Lupe, minimizes Connie's difficulties, and finds faults in Sarah's teaching.*

The case provides a forum for discussing how and what kinds of diversity are valued in the teaching professions. It addresses how decisions about diversity are made, particularly in terms of what kinds of adaptations and accommodations are reasonable for teachers. It also raises issues about how decisions related to successful or unsuccessful teaching are made, especially in the case of persons from underrepresented groups, and whether such decisions can avoid being discriminatory.

53

"I DON'T KNOW. I JUST DON'T THINK YOU CAN BE A TEACHER."

Connie Carlson noticed that it was much quieter in the car this morning as she and her fellow student teachers, Sarah Corbin and Lupe Hernandez, drove to their internship at Birchwood Middle School—certainly quieter than the rides during those first couple of months of their placement. They were thrilled when they had found out that they had been placed not only in the same middle school but also in the same team of teachers in the school, Connie in Language Arts, and Sarah and Lupe both in Social Studies. The three of them had shared so much together over the years—seemingly interminable—at the university and now they were going to share this most important experience of actually teaching, too. Every morning and every afternoon as they carpooled to and from the university, they had lively discussions about new ideas for teaching, reforming education, and overcoming challenges in the classroom. They frequently remarked how their mutual camaraderie and help added immeasurably to the quality of their teacher education program and their student teaching experiences.

But today was different. Dr. Simon, their university supervisor, was coming for an observation seventh period, the time when they team-taught eighth-grade American Studies. Though Connie was always a little nervous when Dr. Simon observed her, that wasn't what she was really worried about. No, it was more important than that. Dr. Simon had also scheduled a meeting for after school with Sarah, Ms. Hakeem, the principal, and Ms. Duckworth, Sarah's cooperating teacher, to talk about Sarah's teaching at Birchwood and whether she should be a teacher. Connie was glad Dr. Simon hadn't asked her to attend the meeting. She didn't think she could stand seeing her friend in such a situation. Sarah was so upset that it had been difficult enough talking with her about it once Dr. Simon made the appointment. She also didn't want Dr. Simon to ask her what she thought about Sarah's being a teacher. Despite all that they had shared and the strong friendship they had, Connie sometimes found herself wondering if Sarah could really be a teacher and she didn't want to have to admit that in front of her.

Three Colleagues

Connie had never known anyone who had disabilities like Sarah's. There had been a few special education kids in her elementary school, but most of the time they were either in separate classrooms or by themselves in the lunchroom and on the playground. Students with learning disabilities had been mainstreamed or integrated—she had learned these terms in her Introduction to Special Education course—into some of her classes in middle school and high school. But she had never encountered a teacher with disabilities before, definitely not any in the small, farming community she grew up in nor any in the city and suburban schools where she had her field experiences in her teacher-training program. Sarah's meeting with Dr. Simon had started her wondering why not, since there were so many students with disabilities receiving special education and since persons with disabilities represented the largest minority group in this country. Didn't any individuals with disabilities ever go into teaching?

Sarah had several disabilities as a result of a stroke seven years ago when she first started college, back before Connie knew her. Sarah was paralyzed on the right side of her body and so used a cane to help her walk. She sometimes had difficulty coming up with the word she wanted in conversations and seemed to hesitate or stutter more in her speech than most people typically do. And she had a learning disability which made reading and writing difficult for her. She had all of her course readings taped for her. She asked classmates, like Connie, for copies of their class notes to supplement the ones she took. She received extra time to take exams and a proctor who would read the questions to her. And—Connie had heard this innumerable times—Sarah had thanked her lucky stars and her vocational rehabilitation counselor for a computer with spelling and grammar checkers that allowed her to produce written work that didn't stand out from everyone else's because of proofreading errors.

Getting to know someone with disabilities like Sarah's had really been important to Connie. Growing up in Moosewood Falls, she had few chances to meet many people who were very different from her, people from some of the minority groups that they learned about in school. The only examples of individuals from cultural groups other than Finns, Swedes, Norwegians, and Germans came from movies, television, videos in school, and their occasional trips to Forest City, the state capital, though actual encounters there were pretty limited. That was one of the strong points about the teacher education program at the university. They had a strong record in attracting students from racial and ethnic minority groups into the program. The cultural diversity brought about by the African-American, Asian-American, Native American, and Hispanic-American students not only added to the richness of the classes but also prepared her more realistically, Connie felt, to work in a multicultural society. And it made it possible for her to become friends with Lupe.

Lupe came from El Paso, Texas, and attended the university through one of the grants that the teacher education program offered to recruit more minorities into teaching. She had been born in Mexico and had spent the first few years of her life there; much of her extended family still lived outside of Guadalajara. Her family had come to this country illegally but then became citizens under an amnesty law years ago. Spanish was still her primary language and, especially when she was excited, she would leave her hesitant and less expressive English behind for a moment, get her ideas out in Spanish, and then provide the translation. Despite Lupe's dramatic hand movements and facial expressions, Connie was glad for that extra step in the conversation as she had still picked up only a little Spanish from Lupe.

Connie, Sarah, and Lupe had learned early on, through the trial and error of working with others in their cohort of teacher education classmates, that they formed a pretty good team whenever their courses called for a small group project. Each appreciated that the others were responsible and pulled their own weight on an assignment, taking their fair shares of the writing and any drudge work like digging in the library. But each also contributed uniquely because of her special talents.

Lupe could bring energy to their work, particularly when they'd start to lose interest partway through the assignment. She could motivate them by pointing out the importance of what they were doing. She was awfully good at seeing implications of social justice in teaching, and she used her insights to spur them on for the last stages of the project. It seemed that the past challenges in her life—the poverty, life in the barrio, and firsthand experiences with blatant discrimination—fueled her own "gusto." Her accounts of her experiences, with all their vivid detail, helped give meaning and a higher purpose to the abstract tasks of assignments.

Sarah's strength was in her creativity. She could see interesting and valuable connections among the materials that each found for their work, connections that helped generate new insights among the three. Her creativity also extended to her skills with technology. Sarah knew more about computers and other devices than probably anyone in their cohort, probably more even than many of the professors. And she knew how to get her hands on the equipment. Many of their class presentations took on a professional look because of her skills and efforts.

And Connie knew she added a logical and analytical component to the group, along with a compulsiveness for details; these contributions weren't as exciting as Lupe's and Sarah's but, according to their professors' comments on their work, they were important nevertheless. She was good at telling when important points in their lessons weren't developed specifically enough, described adequately with examples, or provided with enough practice for the students. At the university, the probing that she would prompt usually led to a better understanding of the topics than they originally expected.

Connie smiled to herself thinking about some of the fun they had had working together and what they had accomplished. Their senses of humor meshed pretty closely, which made those all-nighters more bearable. They learned much from each other. And their cooperation among themselves and support for each other—sometimes two of them would do a little more on a project if the third had a big exam coming up, knowing that she would take an extra share the next time—seemed to model the kinds of collaboration touted in their methods courses.

So Connie had never thought that Sarah couldn't be a teacher until she heard Sarah tearfully relate Dr. Simon's challenges to her choice of a profession. Before, she had just seen her warm, funny, intelligent, creative friend who had a way with kids. Now Dr. Simon's questions kept coming back to her, and she didn't have answers to them. "What are you going to do about reading out loud to your classes or about written materials handed to you at meetings, since you always want everything audiotaped or read to you? What are you going to do when you have to write on the board in class or write notes to other teachers or the principal? What kind of example will you set for your students when you read and write like that? What about all the extra time it takes you to do things? If someone else does all this reading and writing for you, are you still the teacher? Aren't we changing the standards of what it takes to be a teacher too much if we make such accommodations for you? Is it going to be fair to some school district to hire a teacher who has such problems? What's it going to do for the reputations of our teacher education program and the university?"

Connie reached yet another impasse with these tough questions just as they drove into the Birchwood parking lot. Sarah pulled the car into one of the handicapped parking spots, working the hand control for the brakes. Still quiet, they all got out of the car and walked into the school.

The Lesson

When the bell ending sixth period rang, Connie, Sarah, and Lupe left the teachers' lounge. They had spent their prep period going over next period's team-taught lesson one more time, trying to fine-tune it and improve it not only to meet Dr. Simon's observation but also to try to put Sarah in the best light before her meeting after school.

Dr. Simon was waiting for them outside their classroom. He greeted them and entered the classroom after them. Connie watched him head to his customary spot in a back corner of the room, take out his yellow pad of paper and his pencil, and put on his passive observer's face. "How can he look so calm and undisturbed?" she thought. "Doesn't he know how much this meeting is hurting Sarah and us? How could he do such a thing to one of the program's best students?"

When the bell starting seventh period rang, Connie greeted the class and called them to order. As she reviewed the major points from previous lessons and previewed today's topics and activities in the unit on discrimination, she worked with the overhead transparency Sarah had produced last night on her computer; Lupe went around the room collecting work; Sarah took the attendance. As she was placing the attendance card outside the door, a student delivered a message. Sarah read it to herself and then said, "Albert, Ms. Ha-Hakeem would like to speak wwwwith you right now." After Albert got up and left the room, Sarah closed the door.

Lupe's Discussion

Lupe had the first portion of the lesson. She was to lead a class discussion on personal experiences of discrimination and how those experiences felt. Connie made a smooth transition to this activity and went to the side of the room. She loved to sit back and watch Lupe teach, and she could. Even though the typical liveliness of this group of eighth graders was heightened by the fact that this was the last period of the day and that the class was more heterogeneous than most in the school—there were gifted kids, kids from poor families and from wealthy families, kids with a variety of disabilities, and white kids and minority kids—Lupe could get them to do anything she wanted them to do.

Lupe wrote the word *DISCRIMINATION* on the chalkboard. Sarah recalled how Lupe tended not to write much on the board when leading this type of brainstorming discussion, just a few key words from the students' responses and all sorts of lines and marks for connections and emphasis, sort of a shorthand summary of the content and feeling of the interchange. She remembered that Dr. Simon had suggested this approach to Lupe as a way both to keep the momentum of the discussion flowing and to put less of a demand on Lupe's writing of English on the spot. It certainly was effective in Lupe's hands.

"I want you to think about any times you've felt discriminated against because of one of the characteristics that makes you *you*, like because of your gender or your religion. Maybe your race or cultural background. Or it could have been because of your family's income or your abilities or difficulties doing things. I want you to share that experience briefly with us, if you're willing, and then, very important, I want you to tell us how you felt after that experience, what you wanted to do because of it. I'll start as an example."

She told about the time, only a few years ago, when she was in high school, when she and her family were going through the naturalization process with the U. S. Immigration and Naturalization Service. Mexicans applying for naturalization were required not only to take a class which taught them about United States history and the U. S. Constitution, and a certain number of hours of English as a Second Language, but also to go to the INS Office for numerous appointments to "complete paperwork."

The office was open from Monday through Friday, 8:30 a.m. to 3:00 p.m. The first day Lupe and her mother went to the office, after a 50-minute bus ride, they arrived at 7:40. There were 43 people lined up outside the unopened door. Finally, at 8:00, the office was opened, and the people all walked in—in a line as if they'd done this many times before—to the counter where INS employees were stationed at three windows. But the people didn't approach the employees at the windows. They went to the tear-off tablet at the end of the counter to take their "numbers." Lupe and her mother followed and took number 44. They sat. They waited.

"No habia aire in the room! There was no air in the room!" Lupe exclaimed. "El calor! The heat!" Lupe said that by 9:00 she noticed only seven people had been called to the windows. Some of the women waiting for their turn were pregnant and had several small children with them. "Pobrecitos! Poor kids," Lupe said. "They were hot, hungry, and the mothers were desesperada—desperate." Lupe also noticed that every so often someone entered the office and went straight to one of the windows without taking a number. At 3:00, one man came out from a back office to say the office was closed. They were on number 39. "Put your numbers on the counter and come back another day," he said. "Otro dia! Another day!" Lupe had taken off her job at the restaurant to bring her mother. "Otro dia meant two days sin dinero, two days without money!" As she and her mother rode back to the barrio on the bus, they planned to come on Thursday. Wednesday was too important a day to miss tips at the restaurant.

When Lupe got to work on Wednesday, a friend from school, two years older than she, came in for coffee. She brought her baby to show Lupe. She was American, but right after graduation she had left El Paso to live in Chihuahua City with her new husband's family. As they admired and talked to the baby, the friend asked Lupe if she had had to go to the INS office for anything yet. She went on to explain that she had called about getting citizenship papers for her baby. She said, "You know, I've been speaking Spanish exclusively for so long, I automatically began my conversation in Spanish. And then the woman was SO rude and uncooperative that I became furious! I fell back on my English to tell her that I am a U. S. citizen and I know the laws regarding the rights of my baby being a citizen too and that I demanded only the proper paperwork forms to complete! The awful woman backed down and became instantly polite. She said I had to go to that office, but she said something about not 'taking a number' and just going to one of the clerks and saying, 'Ofelia sent me to ask for form EE.' Doesn't that sound weird?"

Lupe thought of her mother, the hot smelly room, the anxious children. "It doesn't sound weird. It sounds racist!"

Everyone in the room was spellbound as Lupe told her story and her reactions. Not only was the content of her narrative stunning but so was the way she related it, modulating the pitch and loudness of her voice, even down to a barely audible whisper, moving all around the room. Nobody said a word when she stopped. After a prolonged pause to let the story sink in a little more, Lupe asked, "Does anyone have an experience he or she would like to share?" Hands shot up, and voices called out to volunteer stories. Lupe worked the class perfectly, always figuring out which student should be the next to call on so as not to lose the student, giving each student just enough time to relate his or her story but not too much to lose the momentum that overtook the class. The rising noise level of students volunteering and calling out their affirmations and comments to one anothers' stories was starting to make Connie feel uncomfortable. Not sure if she should step in and help calm down some of the louder students, she looked back to check Dr. Simon's reaction. His normally inscrutable face was smiling as he was busily writing notes on his pad. She took this to be a sign of his approval for what was transpiring in the class and so decided to stay on the sidelines and let Lupe run the show.

"And time for one last volunteer." Lupe had somehow managed to get every student who wanted to to tell his or her tale of discrimination in this brief part of the class. The shorthand summary on the board— just a jumble of lines and words, including a few in Spanish and some misspelled in English, really did capture the essence of the discussion. Those students who were wise enough to copy it in their notes would be able to recreate at a later date the experience they had just shared.

"And those were some of the things we wanted to do when we felt discriminated against. Now Ms. Corbin will tell you about some of the actions people in this country have taken when they felt discriminated against that led to the laws and court cases you read about in your history reading for today." Lupe provided the segue into Sarah's section of the lesson. Lupe was always a tough act to follow in the classroom and her performance today had been especially strong.

Sarah's Lecture

The kids were pumped. They were talking to each other and moving around in their seats. They wanted more stimulation of the kind they had just received, but Connie knew they weren't going to get it. Few people could match Lupe in this kind of teaching activity, especially not Sarah who, because of her disabilities, used far less dramatic variety in her speaking and limited her classroom movements. And this material on laws and court cases lacked the excitement of these vivid, personal experiences. But the district's curriculum guidelines said this content had to be covered and reviewed several times before the end of the semester. The three of them had decided a long time ago when they planned this unit that one of the review sessions could be in the form of a lecture about the experiences of people who filed suits about discrimination and worked to get antidiscrimination laws passed. They would play off of the students' reactions to discrimination by showing some constructive ways in which people have reacted to this problem in our country. Sarah knew the most about this from the legal history course she had taken. She was also generally good with lectures, as she had to produce detailed outlines in order to deliver them, and she usually provided them to the class via overhead transparencies. This helped those students who had problems making sense out of long lectures. It had seemed like a good idea back then—and Connie thought it still made pedagogical sense—but she wondered about the wisdom of the decision now given the after-school meeting quickly approaching. At one level she was glad she didn't have to follow Lupe, but at another level she was concerned about having her friend do so now.

Connie stood up and took on a more alert status as Sarah turned on the overhead projector and started to bring the class to attention. Connie scanned the classroom, trying to catch any problem behaviors early to help her friend. She saw Lupe on the other side of the room, slowly pacing back and forth with the same intent.

"Cuh-cuh-cuh-class! Class!" Sarah called out to establish order. The quietness of her voice was difficult to hear over the murmuring still in the room so Connie, Lupe, and a few of the students asked for quiet. "The readingsssssssssss from last night fo.. .. ...cussed on laws and lawsuits about di-di-discrimination—I always have a hard time saaaaay-ing that word—dis-crim-i-na-tion. Today's cr-cr-cr. . . ." As Sarah was looking for her word, Connie thought she heard Geoffrey, one of their gifted students, offer "Today's cripple, meaning you?" in something of a stage whisper to his neighbors. She wasn't sure whether that's what he had said, but he looked at Connie right afterwards, as if to see whether she had heard him. Standing as straight as she could, arms folded across her chest, she glared with her strongest teacher look, bristling inside with anger. He bowed his head, his now sheepish face turning bright red as he looked down at his desk. Connie wondered why some of these kids would make cruel remarks like that about Sarah. There seemed to be suspect, smart-aleck remarks every once in a while, usually during one of these lecture situations and often from some of the brighter students in the class. "What are they trying to show," she asked herself, "that they're better than somebody else who can't do some things as well as they can?" Connie knew, though, that many of the kids who had difficulties in the class, particularly the special education kids, seemed to give Sarah better attention than she herself typically got unless she worked especially hard at it. There seemed to be some sort of connection between Sarah and these students. Nancy, the school aide for Tricia, a girl in the class with multiple disabilities who used a wheelchair, also noticed this about her charge. She frequently told Sarah how Tricia would tell her, through the communication board on her wheelchair, that Sarah was her favorite teacher of all time.

Sarah started her lecture by talking about the efforts of Linda Brown to attend white schools in Topeka, Kansas, that led to the 1954 Supreme Court ruling in the case of *Brown v. Board of Education* that overturned the concept of "separate but equal." It always took Sarah a little while to get into the flow of her lectures. She had to focus her attention a lot on what she was doing—lecturing and keeping track of her notes and the overheads—otherwise she might lose her place, and it would take her a while to get it all together again. Connie knew that Sarah especially wanted to avoid that problem today. Consequently, though, Sarah didn't do as much monitoring of her students' attention as she should have, particularly given the lively state they were in after Lupe's teaching. So Connie and Lupe responded to many of the incipient disruptions for her, doing this as subtly as they could, both so they wouldn't interrupt Sarah's lecture and so that Dr. Simon might not notice. Connie glanced his way, though, after one such episode and saw that he was looking at her. He turned to write in his notes, slowly shaking his head.

Sarah talked next about Rosa Parks's refusal to sit in the back of the bus in Montgomery, Alabama, the sit-ins at segregated lunch counters, and the protests led by Dr. Martin Luther King, Jr., and other civil rights leaders that led to the 1964 Civil Rights Act. Connie noticed that Sarah was starting to loosen up more. She was looking up from her notes every now and then and even brought a few students back to attention by quietly mentioning their names as she was lecturing, almost as if she were talking personally to them.

By the time Sarah discussed the activities of Justin Dart and other disability rights activists that led to the passage of the Americans with Disabilities Act of 1990, Connie saw that Sarah was speaking without her notes yet was synchronized perfectly with the outline projected on the overhead at the front of the room. Her quiet voice, though still disfluent at times, made fewer hesitations and mispronunciations. The class was quiet now and attentive.

Connie sensed a lot of emotion in her friend as she talked. There seemed to be a mixture of hurt and anger and pride as she reviewed some of the provisions of the law, like the employment components of the Act that say that employers can't refuse to hire a qualified person with a disability because of the person's disability and that employers must make reasonable accommodations for persons with disabilities. As Sarah closed her portion of the class by relating the story of the successful protest by students at Gallaudet University in 1988 to hire the institution's first deaf president, Connie realized what all this emotion meant. This was Sarah's equivalent to Lupe's story of discrimination earlier, her way of venting some of her feelings over the treatment she had experienced and was even now encountering. And, Connie thought, some of the students were beginning to understand this too.

Connie knew, after all the times she had seen Sarah teach, that Sarah had been at the top of her game today, and she knew that Sarah felt this too. There were still some things that some might consider flaws in her teaching—there probably always would be—such as, how she focused her attention, the imperfections in her speech, her quiet presence, and the slow development of her teaching rhythm. But this was the best she could do and she needed her best for today. The smiles between Connie, Sarah, and Lupe as Connie took her place at the front of the room to begin her teaching conveyed this message among the three friends.

Connie's Turn

Connie felt good as she got the students ready for the English portion of the lesson by asking them to take out their copies of *To Kill a Mockingbird*. The tension about Sarah's meeting after school was relieved when she saw her colleague's teaching performance today. Also, the students seemed to be picking up the theme of this lesson—experiences of discrimination and how people respond to them—after Lupe's discussion and Sarah's lecture. Now Connie was going to play one more variation on that theme before they let the class have some time to work on their small group presentations, which were due in two weeks.

Connie had told the students to read up to at least the start of the trial. She planned to lead the students in a discussion of when Atticus Finch truly realized the discrimination that had been so rampant in his town and to ask what they thought he was going to do about it. She had her notes all ready, listing possible scenes the students might suggest and some questions she could ask to challenge the thinking behind their choices of events.

"So when do you think Atticus was finally sure, real sure, that there was lots of discrimination going on in the town?" Connie posed the question and started to count silently to herself, almost a reflex with her now, to allow enough time for her students to generate thoughtful answers. "Fifteen, sixteen, seventeen," she was thinking. Not one hand was raised. "Well, when do you think he knew about the discrimination, let's say, only against his family?" She looked at her students. Many were thumbing through their paperbacks; others seemed to be trying to read pages of the book quickly. No one was looking up at her so as not to be mistaken as ready to volunteer a response. "How about the Halloween episode? Remember? Scout's attacked and there's all that chicken wire and she's real scared? And Boo comes to the rescue? Anybody remember that?" Some of the bent heads nodded slightly. Connie didn't want to tell them all the possible times; that would be too much like a lecture and contrary to the Whole Language philosophy she believed in. She couldn't tell whether the students hadn't kept up with the reading or whether they didn't understand her, and she had become too flustered with this extensive silence and Dr. Simon in the back of the room to think of some way to resolve the problem.

"Well, since you can't seem to figure this out now, and we're using up a lot of our valuable time, this is what I'll have you do. By tomorrow, I want each of you to be able to tell me one scene that shows that Atticus knows about at least some of the discrimination and to be able to tell me how you know he knows. And be ready to be able to write all of that down, just in case there's a pop quiz. Let's spend the last 20 minutes working on our small group projects." Groans arose in the classroom, and a few of the books were tossed to desk tops in disgust. Connie made the last decision without consulting with her colleagues, but it was the next activity on the lesson plan, and her part of the lesson looked like it was going nowhere. She knew Lupe and Sarah would back her up if Dr. Simon called her on it. She felt angry with herself for making that threat about the quiz, a threat which she had no intention of following through, but she had never been stymied like this before during a lesson, and she was especially chagrined that it had occurred today with Dr. Simon here and the appointment after school. "Maybe he'll replace me with Sarah in that meeting and question whether I should be a teacher," she thought.

Group Work

Connie, Lupe, and Sarah had divided the class into heterogeneous cooperative groups for this project, a group presentation on historical, legal, and social issues involved in discrimination. The group had flexibility in determining specific content they would cover and the form the presentation would take, with the one proviso that everyone in the group had to present something. They felt they had distributed the diversity in the class pretty well among the groups. During the group work time today, Sarah was going to help a group that had determined they wanted to use some computer equipment for their talk. She and a couple of students had borrowed the equipment from the school's media center and set it up in the room at lunchtime. Lupe offered to work with the group that was the furthest behind on the assignment as the deadline was rapidly approaching. They had barely gotten beyond the first stage in their planning. Connie was to be the floater, keeping on top of the management of the classroom overall and assisting groups if problems arose.

As Connie walked around and monitored the classroom, she was careful not to look at Dr. Simon. After seeing his reactions to Sarah's smaller problems earlier, she wanted to put off his reaction to her major difficulty as long as possible. She watched Lupe and her students over at the side of the room. She could see her working the same kind of influence over them that she sometimes did over Sarah and her; the kids' heads were nodding, eyes were lighting up with ideas, and several were trying to talk at once. Connie thought that they probably didn't have to worry about that group anymore though they should check on them each day.

Connie looked over toward Sarah and her group at the back of the room with all of their equipment. She was showing Geoffrey how to use a HyperCard stack on the Macintosh to drive the videodisc player so he could select and edit portions of the ABC videodisc on the civil rights movement for the group's talk, creating a montage of actual, historical news footage to illustrate their points. Connie could not know what was happening just by looking at it, but Sarah had told her yesterday after school when they were planning what she'd be doing with the group. A little later Connie watched Sarah's group again. This time Sarah was showing the group, on another computer, what she had set up to help them realize their plan for having Tricia "speak" her part of the presentation herself. Tricia was going to dictate her speech to a student in the group, using her communication board. Then the student would type the speech into the computer. When it was time for the presentation, Tricia would push a key on the computer's keyboard, getting a speech synthesizer to say Tricia's speech to the class, thus allowing Tricia to recite a presentation out loud herself for the first time ever. Tricia couldn't wait to get started, and her scribe had a difficult time keeping up with the message she was communicating with her board.

The group project time went quickly and without incident. A few minutes before the bell was to ring, Lupe called the students back together as a class to summarize the day's lesson and activities and to preview tomorrow's class and how these parts related to the whole unit. The bell rang, the students left, and Connie, Lupe, and Sarah waited, with a wide range of emotions, to talk to Dr. Simon.

Dr. Simon's Observations

"We don't have too much time to talk about my observations because of the meeting Sarah and I have in a few minutes, so let's get started," Dr. Simon said. "Lupe, that was a great lesson! Your story was so moving. It really gave the class's activities a strong start. Your use of that summarizing technique on the board that we had talked about before was good as usual. I think it helped the students a lot. You might think, too, about having the students write out their experiences right after you tell your story if you ever use this lesson again. Then they can read their stories back to the class. That'll give you more time to summarize their remarks in English, with enough time to think about the spellings if you're a bit unsure."

"Connie," Dr. Simon said—she could almost hear the axe starting its descent—"every teacher has lessons like the one you had today so don't get too bent out of shape by it. You thought pretty well on your feet, though lay off the punitive remarks. I think they didn't really understand what you wanted. Another idea for starting, or rescuing, a discussion like that would be to have the students think of one concrete image of discrimination in the book, list those on the board, and then move into your ideas about figuring out when Atticus knew. Or, maybe break them up into smaller groups—this was the third large group activity in a row—giving each of them a particular scene to analyze in terms of what Atticus was thinking and feeling at the time. Mostly, though, just shake off the self-doubts and learn from the experience. I still think you'll make a fine teacher." Connie was shocked. She was sure she was going to get chewed out. She was also surprised that Dr. Simon seemed to know what she was feeling. And she thought his suggestions were awfully good, too.

"And, Sarah, you still have problems with classroom management. It was nice of your friends to take care of the disruptions for you, but that won't happen in the real world. You need a stronger presence up there. Can't you talk any louder when you're teaching?"

"YES," Sarah fairly boomed out. Connie and Lupe were surprised at the volume of Sarah's voice but doubted she would be able to keep that up for a whole class period, let alone a whole day of teaching.

"That's better. I knew you could do it. Now just keep your voice raised, and that'll keep those kids in line. You're still having problems with that slow start to your teaching, too. You're going to have to figure out some way to get over that." He looked at the clock on the wall. "Well, we'd better get going, Sarah. We don't want the others to have to wait for us."

Connie was livid. This was ALL that Dr. Simon had to say about Sarah's teaching today! Pointing out problems with classroom management and a slow start! Where had he been? What had he been doing when Sarah was teaching? Hadn't he picked up on the feeling in the room at the end of her lesson? Hadn't he felt it himself? She wondered if maybe his purpose for observing Sarah wasn't so much to help her become the best teacher she could be—and Connie believed, especially after today, that Sarah would be a wonderful teacher—but to look for evidence to support his own assumptions about Sarah's capabilities. Whatever his reasons—saving the prestige of the almighty program and university, protecting his narrow ideas about how a teacher should be, or saving himself the extra work it would take to give Sarah all the help she needed—she couldn't tell; but whatever it was, she doubted it would be adequate, at least for her.

Connie and Lupe watched their friend gather her book bag and her cane and leave to catch up with Dr. Simon, who was already walking a few steps ahead. As they started down the hall, they could see Dr. Simon shaking his head and hear him sigh, "I don't know, Sarah. I just don't think. . . ."

QUESTIONS TO CONSIDER

1. Considering what you know about Sarah, what do you think about her being a teacher? Why?

2. How would you answer Dr. Simon's questions to Sarah? Is there any other information you would want to know before answering?

3. In efforts to promote diversity in the teaching profession, are some types of diversity to be sought and valued, for instance, the type of cultural diversity that Lupe provides, and other types, like Sarah's dis-

ability, to be avoided or discouraged? In other words, are there advantages to some types of diversity and disadvantages to others? What are some of them?

4. Who should make the choices about which diversities to value and how?

5. If you were Connie or Lupe, what would you say to Sarah in the car on the way home?

6. Have your views about Sarah becoming a teacher changed at all? Why?

7. Should we support people who represent diversity in our society in the teaching profession? What kinds of support do we provide now? What additional kinds of support should we provide, if any? Is there ever a point at which we can provide too much support? Are these kinds of supports fair to those who don't need them or who can't receive them? Why or why not?

8. How can we tell when someone, especially someone who is different from society's majority for whatever reason—such as gender, race, ethnicity, disability, or sexual preference—should not be a teacher? Can we avoid discriminating against that person because of his or her difference? How?

RECOMMENDED READINGS

Cochran-Smith, M. (1991). Learning to teach against the grain. *Harvard Educational Review,* 61: 279–310; and Martin, R. J. (1991). The power to empower: Multicultural education for student-teachers. In C. E. Sleeter (ed.), *Empowerment through multicultural education.* Albany: State University of New York Press.

> These two writings address critical advocacy and ways of changing the "narrowness" of some approaches to teaching.

Fuller, M. L. (1992). Teacher education programs and increasing minority school populations: An educational mismatch? In C. A. Grant (ed.), *Research and multicultural education: From the margins to the mainstream.* London: The Falmer Press.

> Fuller discusses issues concerning the recruitment and retention of teachers from minority groups that are pertinent to this case.

Gerber, P. J. (1992). Being learning disabled, a beginning teacher and teaching a class of students with learning disabilities. *Exceptionality,* 3: 213–231.

> This case study of a beginning learning disabilities teacher who has learning disabilities himself provides both descriptions of his experiences as a teacher and insights into the difficulties he faced and the successes he achieved.

Gilmore, J., Merchant, D., & Moore, A. (1980). *Educators with disabilities: A resource guide.* Washington, DC: American Association of Colleges for Teacher Education. (ERIC Document Reproduction Service No. ED 240 304.)

This seminal work in the research on educators who have disabilities is based on a survey of more than 900 educators. This guide also contains suggestions for developing accommodations.

Keller, C. E., Karp, J. M., & Simula, V. L. (1992, February). *Examining the experiences of educators who have disabilities: Implications for enhancing diversity in teacher education programs.* (ERIC Document Reproduction Service No. ED 342 744.)

Paper presented at the annual meeting of the American Association of Colleges for Teacher Education, San Antonio, TX. The research described in this paper identifies factors that make for successful and unsuccessful experiences for educators with disabilities. It also suggests an alternative to the gatekeeper model commonly used in teacher education that might be more facilitative for persons with disabilities.

Long, J. C. (1992, February). *Learning disabled student teachers.* Paper presented at the annual meeting of the American Association of Colleges for Teacher Education, San Antonio, TX; and Yanok, J. (1987). Equal opportunity in teacher education programs for the learning disabled. *Journal of Teacher Education,* 38: 48–52.

Long and Yanok discuss the implications of Section 504 of the Rehabilitation Act of 1973 and of the litigation that interprets this law for teacher education programs.

McGee, K. A., & Kauffman, J. M. (1989). Educating teachers with emotional disabilities: A balance of private and public interests. *Teacher Education and Special Education,* 12: 110–116.

These authors present a probing analysis of the issues involved in dealing with educators who have mental health problems.

U. S. Equal Employment Opportunity Commission (1992, January). *A technical assistance manual on the employment provisions (Title D of the Americans with Disabilities Act).* Washington, DC: U. S. Government Printing Office.

This manual is invaluable for explaining, especially with clear examples, the employment requirements of the Americans with Disabilities Act.

READ MY LIPS—NO SIGN LANGUAGE IN SPEECH CLASS!

DEBRA ECKERMAN PITTON

ABSTRACT

This case identifies the struggle that faces Sarah, a middle school speech teacher, as she explores her philosophy regarding inclusion. Also addressed is the issue of support, or lack of support, which is offered to teachers when they attempt to improve their practice and change their methodology. In addition, this case presents the need for constant reflection by teachers as they work to mesh their philosophy with their practice.

Sarah unintentionally initiates a conflict with her innocent request to a hearing-impaired student. Upon receiving a memo from Bonnie, the resource teacher, Sarah is informed that she is violating the rights of a student, Marie, by asking when Marie will be ready to speak in class. Sarah bases her actions on prior experience and is concerned that allowing the use of sign language within the structure of a speech communication class will jeopardize her speech curriculum. How this educator wrestles with her belief that the classroom should be a place where everyone is welcome and feels invited and her concern that sign language is not a viable means for communication within a speech class is the focus of Sarah's case study. Imbedded within this account is an emphasis upon reflection as a means for achieving the paradigm shift, or change of perspective, that must occur before teachers can truly model inclusivity.

Read My Lips—No Sign Language in Speech Class!

The Letter

Sarah stood by her desk as she opened her mail. It was the second day of school at the middle school where she taught, and she felt that the semester had begun successfully. She thought about how she had asked the students in her basic speech class to interview another person and then introduce their partner to the rest of the class. The students had appeared comfortable with this low-key activity. Speech was not required here; it was one of the semester-long elective courses that were available for students. Seventh and eighth graders could sign up, although many preferred to take a foreign language or shop. Sarah knew that even though her students had made the choice to take speech, many felt nervous and apprehensive about talking in front of each other. Still, no one had refused to participate yesterday, and that was a good sign.

Although she had spent her first two years at a high school in another district, Sarah had been excited to join the middle school staff when her marriage brought her into this community. She was responsible for the speech curriculum, and another teacher handled theater. She was supposed to be a member of an elective team, but all of the elective instructors' schedules were so varied that no one had a common planning period. Sarah didn't mind; she was so busy that it was easier to dispense with the team effort and work independently. She was pleased that this position at the middle school enabled her to work with young people who were experiencing their first course work in oral communication. The school she taught in was part of a large suburban school district in the Southwest with a predominantly white student population of 1,016 students in the sixth through eighth grades. There was only a 5% minority population in this school. Speech was an elective, but all students took a six-week introduction course in sixth grade, and many returned for basic and the advanced speech classes. Sarah had always kept her enrollment numbers up. The competitive speech team at the high school was extremely successful, and Sarah was attempting to provide a strong feeder program for the ninth through twelfth grade forensic activities.

Sarah continued to glance through the usual notices and memos that filled her mail slot and then opened an envelope marked "confidential." Inside was a notice from the special education resource teacher stating that a complaint had been lodged against Sarah for discrimination. In a state of total surprise, Sarah read the notice that described PL 94–142 and stated that, by law, she must allow Marie, a hearing-impaired student, to give her speeches in sign language. Forcing a student to communicate in a manner that was not the individual's usual method of communication was discriminatory, the letter stated. The notice concluded with a request for a conference by the resource teacher. Sarah was dumbfounded. How could this have happened?

Sarah's Philosophy

A four-year veteran of teaching speech classes, Sarah believed that all young people needed an opportunity to develop confidence in speaking. Her speech classes involved a progression from the basic theory of communication and listening skills to interpersonal communication and the presentation of various types of speeches. Debate was included in the advanced speech course. Even though her students were young and might not give the most complex speeches, Sarah believed that the students' self-confidence and self-esteem were enhanced as they gradually gave more and more challenging presentations in front of their peers. Sarah felt strongly about the importance of her subject area and bristled when anyone hinted that speech class was not really a vital part of the curriculum.

When asked to identify her philosophy of education, Sarah stated, "In today's world everyone has to be able to communicate effectively. Relationships with friends and family, working in groups to solve problems, talking to employees or customers all necessitate that the speaker feel comfortable and capable in delivering his or her message. The students in speech learn how to solve problems by discussing and presenting their viewpoints in a logical fashion. After they take a speech class, students are more comfortable using content knowledge from other areas and talking or presenting on a topic. They can ask and respond to questions with more confidence. One of my objectives as I teach any speech class is that the students realize that communicating and listening to each other is a way to get past the differences that separate many of us, to help students recognize that good communication is respectful of everyone else's point of view. What could be a more vital component in a curriculum for today's society? My philosophy echoes that of the social reconstructionist. I think that if students learn to communicate effectively with all groups of individuals they will also develop the critical thinking skills that will enable them to examine the flaws in our social structure."

The Confrontation

Later that day, Sarah sat in the office of the resource teacher listening as she received further information regarding the complaint that Marie had voiced regarding Sarah. Bonnie, the resource teacher, said that Marie had been in to see her immediately after her first speech class yesterday. An eighth-grade student who had transferred into the school this year, Marie was hearing-impaired and had an interpreter, assigned by the district, who accompanied her at school. Bonnie told Sarah that Marie was upset by the fact that she'd been told that she would have to speak in the speech class.

"But that is not what I said," Sarah responded. "I have had other hearing-impaired students in my classes. Just last year I worked with Carrie, and she didn't have any complaints. Carrie wanted to improve her ability to speak clearly, and I adjusted my requirements so that she could be evaluated fairly. I wasn't planning on grading Marie in the same fashion as everyone else in class. When I spoke with her after class, I merely said that when she was ready to speak in class, she should let me know. What is speech class all about anyway? The definition I have always used is that speech instruction is attempting to improve one's ability to communicate through the spoken word. I realize that Marie has an interpreter and that Carrie used hearing aids and chose to speak for herself. But how am I supposed to evaluate someone in a speech class who doesn't speak?"

Bonnie, a 20-year veteran teacher, reiterated to Sarah that Marie was entitled by law to use her usual communication process and that Marie's choice was sign language. Marie did not have to speak in class. Bonnie said that by suggesting that there would be a time when Marie might be required to speak, Sarah was denying Marie her rights. Bonnie also pointed out that Marie was deaf and that Carrie, a previous student, had been hearing-impaired. This difference, she noted, would create the need for some additional accommodations on Sarah's part.

Sarah left the meeting feeling discouraged and disheartened. She had prided herself on creating an atmosphere where her students learned to discuss and accept differences, and now she was being accused of denying a student's rights. "But how am I supposed to evaluate someone for speaking and listening when they aren't doing any of those activities?" she wondered.

Working It Out

During class that day, Sarah attempted to mend fences. She called Marie over and said that she understood that Marie preferred to use sign language, and that was fine. However, Sarah stated that as this particular course focused on developing speaking and listening skills, it would be very difficult for Marie to participate in the learning activities. She asked Marie about her reasons for taking the class. Marie responded through her interpreter that she wanted to be able to get up in front of the class and give presentations and not be nervous. Sarah suggested that Marie might prefer to take drama, where she could accomplish her goals in an environment where body language and movement were a key factor in the presentations and pantomime was utilized extensively. Marie said nothing in response, and Sarah urged her to see the counselor about a schedule change.

The next day, Sarah found another request for a meeting with Bonnie. "Now what?" she wondered. Bonnie closed the door after Sarah entered and stated that she thought Sarah had understood yesterday that Marie was to be allowed to use sign language during speech class. Sarah recounted her conversation with Marie, and then Bonnie told Sarah to reevaluate her methods of teaching the class to determine an alternate method of evaluating Marie using sign language, because Marie really wanted to take speech, not drama. Bonnie suggested that Sarah call someone from the speech department at the local university to see what they would recommend in this situation.

Finding Resources

During her prep period, Sarah followed up on the suggestion Bonnie had made and phoned the university's speech department. A professor who took her call was very helpful, responding that she often had signing students in her classes who used interpreters. Sarah said that she felt that she would be evaluating the interpreter and not the student in this situation. "When I listen to a discussion group or a formal speech, the students work on tone of voice and pitch, as well as volume and vocal variety. How can I grade this student on those key concepts of the course if she is not doing any of the speaking herself? How will I know if what she is saying is what her written speech really says?" The university professor said that in her experience, interpreters were a mouthpiece and said exactly what the hearing-impaired individual signed. She also said that there were a variety of nuances to sign language that could be misinterpreted. Acknowledging that she found it difficult, the professor suggested that Sarah evaluate only the written component of the speech and focus on the nonverbal communication. Sarah thought of several of her objectives for the class: that students develop the ability to speak clearly, to listen accurately, to present a reading with vocal variety and expression, and to write and present speeches of increasing complexity. If the objectives were only for the student to write a speech that would be delivered by someone else and to develop nonverbal skills, the course would not amount to much.

Sarah spent that night trying to decide what to do. She wondered why Marie felt so opposed to taking a drama class. Sarah pondered the objectives and determined that the course would certainly be an easy one for Marie. The first unit focused on listening skills, and she couldn't participate in any of those activities. Then there was interpersonal communication. Who would be able to talk to Marie besides the interpreter? The next assignment was a short oral interpretation selection, reading literature with expressiveness. If the interpreter did the reading, who would be evaluated? Sarah thought back to the comments she had often heard from teachers and students about how "easy" speech class was compared to other courses in the middle school. "Now that I have to give a grade for someone who is not even speaking in class, I will never be able to get other teachers to see the value of what I do." She sighed. "I know that the rights of the students are important, yet I don't see how I can adjust my course to fit Marie's needs and still provide Marie with a valid learning experience. I will be compromising the standards of the course for Marie, and I really believe that Marie would benefit more from a different type of communication class. What should I do?"

When Sarah returned to class the next day, she noted that Marie's attitude was decidedly reserved. Resigned to the fact that the law was on Marie's side, Sarah told Marie to participate as best she could, and began a listening activity. Throughout all the exercises that day, Marie's interpreter signed to Marie. Was the interpreter telling Marie what was going on? How could the interpreter explain all the various exchanges the students were involved in during class? Sarah noticed that she felt uncomfortable with the fact that anything she said was repeated a few seconds later in sign language. Was the interpreter presenting Sarah's statements accurately?

Reevaluating

Over the course of the next few weeks, Sarah engaged her students in listening-improvement activities and followed up with a listening test. Each day the interpreter and Marie engaged in a lengthy exchange. On the day of the exam Sarah was going to tell Marie that she could go to the library during the test time, but Marie indicated that she wanted to take the test. Her interpreter signed the questions as dictated by Sarah, and Marie diligently wrote her answers. Sarah had to chuckle as the interpreter tried to sign the various sound effects the students were identifying from a recording, but Marie ended up with a perfect paper!

Now Sarah was more confused than ever. If the objective for improving listening was to respond accurately to oral directions and identify specific statements and sounds, and Marie had scored a perfect paper, had Marie met the objective? The interpreter had actually listened to the sounds, but she had presented them to Marie via sign language, and Marie had "listened" accurately. Sarah wondered about the interactions that occurred between the interpreter and Marie. Was Marie exhibiting "listening behavior" in a format that Sarah was unfamiliar with and couldn't observe? "Is my interpretation of listening and speaking the absolute and sole definition?" she mused.

In the interpersonal communication unit that followed, students were assigned to groups. Sarah placed Marie and the other students in groups randomly, telling them that their objective would be to develop and demonstrate techniques for communicating with a variety of individuals in conflict situations. Using problematic scenarios, the groups were to discuss the situation and come up with an answer or choice of action that all group members agreed upon. Marie and her interpreter were right in the middle of the exchange in her group, with Marie frantically nodding her head and alternately smiling and frowning while signing. Sarah noticed that the students were looking at Marie when the interpreter "spoke" for her. She was surprised that they did not seem distracted by the interpreter.

To evaluate this unit, students wrote entries into communication logs each night to express how their group had functioned. As Sarah read these reactions, she was struck by the high degree of respect for different opinions that was commented on by every member of Marie's group. Was this a coincidence, or did Marie's presence contribute to this? Wasn't that what mainstreaming advocates always preached, that students interacting with the handicapped in everyday settings would develop a greater ability to work and play comfortably with diverse individuals? Sarah had to acknowledge that Marie did seem to be using nonverbal skills to enhance her interactions and that her group was demonstrating tolerance for one another's ideas as well as effectively and cooperatively coming to consensus. Again Sarah wondered about the possibility of Marie meeting the objective. After all, Marie relied on an interpreter to communicate. Marie did not actually do the speaking herself. So how could Marie 'speak' to her group? Did she really communicate effectively? How could Sarah tell if Marie used nonthreatening tones or appropriate language? As the instructor, how could she evaluate Marie? Sarah wondered why this issue was such a stumbling block for herself. She thought that perhaps she was so determined to make the speech class a solid academic course that perhaps she was limiting her definition of the concepts of "speech" and "communication."

Sarah remembered that when she had been in an education class during college and they had discussed multicultural and diversity issues in the classroom, she had been very vocal in her support of fairness in the classroom and adamant in her views that we need to be accepting of all individuals. What had happened? Digging through some old college papers, Sarah read an essay she had written on how to create an inclusive environment in a speech class. She had written about how everyone's field of experience was different and that we must try to see things from other people's perspectives, not just our own. Sarah knew that she needed to analyze her own reactions to the current situation. She had been willing to affirm her students' diversity as long as her personal concepts of excellence and equity were not being challenged. Were the standards that she had established for her speech classes inflexible and rigid? Rereading her earlier writings, Sarah was determined to reassess her response to Marie and to rethink her position regarding her curriculum.

A Change of Heart

The objective for the next unit in speech required that the students select and prepare an oral interpretation to read to the class using good vocal techniques. Despite her earlier resolve, as the students engaged in pitch and volume exercises, Sarah found herself doubting that there would be much to evaluate Marie on for this assignment. After all, an oral interpretation was to convey the author's thoughts and feelings through the presentation, and it would again be the interpreter speaking for Marie. When the time came for Marie to give her speech, Sarah wondered how much she would be able to write on the critique sheet if she could only evaluate nonverbal skills. Still, she tried to have an open mind. Marie stood in the center of the room, with her interpreter sitting off to the side, facing the class. Marie presented a short story about a girl's relationship with her little sister. Eyes bright and face full of feeling, Marie delivered her presentation. The conclusion of the story revealed that the bond between the two girls was special because "my sister is deaf."

After the speech, Sarah sat quietly for a moment and then began to write her critique. She commented that Marie needed to slow down some of her signs to allow for the audience to follow her delivery more effectively, and that she should position herself forward and keep her hands at chest height so that the audience could see her gestures. The students had definitely reacted to the presentation; it seemed that Marie had indeed conveyed the author's meaning of that story. After class, Sarah complimented Marie on her presentation. Marie smiled, glanced at her critique and noted that she had rushed her delivery a bit because she was nervous. Sarah told her to try taking a few deep breaths before she began and suggested that she should pause at the end of each sentence for a few more seconds. Marie nodded and added that she was feeling more comfortable speaking in the class.

Later, Sarah stopped in to see Bonnie in the resource room. "I feel like kicking myself," she told the older teacher. "I just had a conversation with Marie about her speech that dealt with specific components of the delivery just as I do with all the other students. If speech involves speaking, and Marie 'spoke' to us with her delivery today, then I guess she is meeting the objectives of the course. Why can't I let go of this vision that speeches can only be presented one way, that oral communication can only be relayed in one form? I know that I can adjust my objectives for Marie, and I have to admit that for her, speech is on a different level. She told me today that she was feeling more comfortable speaking in class. Who am I to disregard Marie's method of speech? I realize that I need to be open to all forms of communication, but I thought I was! It is hard for me to change this perception of how my subject should be presented. I have always been involved in speech outcomes that focused on the oral aspect of communication. I know that I can make adjustments for Marie, but it bothers me that I just can't seem to get past the idea that speech really should include verbal components. Why is it so hard for me to make this shift in thinking? The gap between knowing what is right and feeling totally accepting of the concept is a hard one to bridge."

Bonnie smiled and said that she had known Sarah would come around. "If you need any more help with this issue, just let me know," she told the young speech teacher. As Sarah left the resource teacher's office, she sighed. There has got to be an easier way to reach a conclusion about how far an inclusive curriculum should go before it becomes ineffective for the student involved. Bonnie was just the catalyst; I had to do all the soul-searching.

Sarah shook her head. "I guess that I have just begun to understand what it means to create a truly inclusive classroom. I only wish that as I continue to learn and grow as an educator, I could move forward a little less painfully next time!"

QUESTIONS TO CONSIDER

1. What are the key issues found in this teaching situation? Which are the most urgent?

2. Do you agree with the adjustments that Sarah made in her expectations that allowed Marie to participate in the course? Should Sarah have expanded her options for Marie even more?

/ **3.** How do you think Marie will benefit from taking this course?

/ **4.** What do you think would have happened if the school had supported Sarah's idea and put Marie in another class? How would such a decision affect Marie? Sarah?

5. How might the other teachers, principal, and school board react upon hearing about Marie's complaint of discrimination?

6. How would you feel about having a student with an interpreter in your class? Do you see disadvantages? Advantages?

/ **7.** How do you account for the contradiction between Sarah's stated philosophy and her actions?

8. Could the population of the school and community and the connection with the high school's competitive speech team have contributed to Sarah's views on individual rights and her reaction to this situation? If so, how?

9. Sarah herself stated that one of her objectives was to have students learn to communicate in a manner that was accepting of one another's differences. Why then was it difficult for Sarah herself to accept someone who was different in the case of a student using an interpreter in her speech class?

10. What do you think about Bonnie's reaction to Sarah? How do you think Bonnie views this situation?

11. What do Sarah's comments tell us about her view of the relationship between Bonnie and herself? Do you think Sarah's views are accurate? Is there any way Bonnie and Sarah could create a relationship that would more effectively facilitate their discussions?

12. How do you see yourself dealing with a similar situation where you are asked to react in a way that opposes your view of teaching? Can you provide an example that will facilitate your exploration of this issue?

13. How can you create connections with colleagues to provide yourself with a support system as you face similar situations?

RECOMMENDED READINGS

Adler, A., Rosenfeld, L., & Towne, N. (1989). *Interplay: The process of interpersonal communication.* Chicago: Holt, Rinehart and Winston.
   This book presents the various components of interpersonal communication and identifies methods for improving verbal interactions.

Biehler, R., & Snowman, J. (1993). *Psychology applied to teaching,* (7th ed.). Boston: Houghton Mifflin.
   This text includes chapters dealing with inclusivity in the classroom, with focus on special needs students and their rights as well as teacher

responsibilities, and the psychological rationale for laws such as the American Disabilities Act.

George, P., & Alexander, W. (1993). *The exemplary middle school.* New York: Harcourt Brace Jovanovich.

The philosophy of the middle school is identified in this text, with focus on the needs of students of this age group: the age of transience.

Johnson, J., & Johnson, R. (1991). *Joining together.* Englewood Cliffs, NJ: Prentice-Hall.

Understanding the processes of communication within and between groups and individuals is discussed in this text, as well as strategies for dealing with conflict situations.

Samovar, L., & Porter, R. (1991). *Communication between cultures.* Belmont, CA: Wadsworth.

This text defines multicultural communication and presents a view of the difficulties of communicating across cultures.

Samovar, L., & Porter, R. (1991). *Intercultural communication.* Belmont, CA: Wadsworth.

The readings in this text present an overview of specific communication concerns identified by various cultures and subcultures, as well as methods for improving intercultural communication. Chapter three includes an essay by Kathy Jankowski specifically focused on communicating with deaf individuals.

MARY ANTINI: TEACHER, COUNSELOR, OR PROSECUTOR?

CHERYL SANDORA

ABSTRACT

The growing diversity of students in our schools has led to an increased emphasis on multicultural literature. A culturally diverse approach to teaching requires that teachers be better prepared and possess an awareness of the needs of individual students. This case study examines problems that arise when a teacher, new to her school and geographical setting, uses a multicultural approach in her language arts classes. During a discussion of the ideal family, one of her students reveals that her biological father is her brother, and that her grandfather is abusing her sexually. The study includes suggested approaches to dealing with this case from an instructional perspective. It concludes with a series of questions designed to stimulate discussion of educators' responsibilities to their students.

83

Mary Antini: Teacher, Counselor, or Prosecutor?

Mary Antini had recently relocated to one of the southern states from a northeastern city where she had taught in an urban setting for five years. When she accepted a teaching position in this small rural community, she knew there would be differences and asked her new colleagues for some advice. They told her of the many positives including the students' respectful responses of "Yes, ma'am" and "No, ma'am." They also warned her of problems due to the high incest rate. Though Mary knew there would be some problems, she felt confident she would make a successful transition. Mary considered herself an excellent English teacher and felt her strong pedagogical knowledge combined with her sensitivity to individuals made her an ideal candidate for that role.

Mary was teaching eighth- and ninth-grade English/Language Arts at Leyola Middle School. Her two ninth-grade classes were the lowest of the four levels in the school. Her three eighth-grade classes were advanced, which was one level below honors. In her second-period ninth-grade class was a very popular student, Ron. Ron was a top athlete in the school, playing basketball, football, and baseball. He was not only an exceptional athlete but also a charming student who was well liked by other students, teachers, and administrators. Everyone loved Ron.

This second-period class consisted of only 15 students. Twelve students were African-American (6 male and 6 female), and 3 were white (all female). Mary, who strongly believed she saw students as individuals and never as colors, had no problem with the makeup of this class. In fact, Mary's goal in every class was to teach more than just English or language arts. She would strive to teach acceptance, not just acceptance of cultural diversities, but acceptance of all diversities. Because of this belief, Mary's prereading lessons usually focused on an issue which would be the impetus for a discussion on diversity of some kind.

On this day, the students were to read "Forgiveness in Families" by Alice Munro. Prior to reading the story, Mary had her students write down what they believed to be an ideal "family." Mary was hoping to spark a discussion on various cultures and their family customs. The students cooperated as usual, and the discussion was going well until Mary asked Ron for his idea of "family." Ron was usually waiting eagerly to answer, but today was different. Mary asked Ron to share his response. At first, he pretended he misunderstood the activity. "Oh, I am sorry Mrs. A. I thought you asked us what we thought the family in the story would be like." Mary accepted that excuse but then pushed him to think again about an ideal family. "OK, Ron, now that you know what we're looking for, share with us your idea of the ideal family." Ron adamantly stated, "I have no definition for family, and I don't care to think of one." Because Mary had a good relationship with Ron, she probed further for a response. "Oh, come on, Ron. I have never known you not to have an opinion on anything." Again, Ron refused to answer. "I said I don't have an answer, and I don't feel like thinking of one." This time Mary sensed hostility and backed off. After class, however, Mary stopped Ron at the door and asked him if there was a problem. Without even looking at Mary, Ron mumbled, "I'm just not feeling well," and left the room. Mary was bothered by this situation as it was so out of character for Ron, and she sensed there was something more than he was telling.

The next morning before school began, a young girl named Janine entered Mary's classroom and asked for two weeks of work for Ron. Because Ron was also very popular with the ladies, Mary assumed this beautiful little girl who reminded her of Janet Jackson was his girlfriend. Mary asked Janine what the problem was, and Janine explained that her family had taken Ron to the hospital the previous evening where he was diagnosed with pneumonia. It was then that Mary realized this was Ron's sister. Again, Mary was surprised. She had never heard Ron mention having a sister, and certainly the two looked nothing alike. But then Mary reminded herself that she was one of seven children, no two resembling each other.

Ten days later Ron returned to school with his usual abundance of energy. He came to see Mary before school had begun just to let her know of his return. "Hey, Mrs. A, I'm back. Did you miss me?" Mary assured Ron that not only did she miss him but that the students were ready to take the class to his home. Ron stated, "Well, it's a good thing you didn't. My family doesn't like company. All I did was sit around and catch up on my soaps." Mary laughed and said, "Now, Ron, with all of that work I sent, you are telling me that you had time to watch television? Well I'll remember that the next time you are home sick." Mary told Ron that she was surprised to have met his sister, since he had never mentioned her, and commented on what a beautiful girl she was. Ron became uncomfortable and immediately left the room. Again, Mary sensed she was missing something, but she let it go, since it was his first day back at school.

Ron's comment about his family and his strong reaction at the mention of his sister reminded Mary again about the last day Ron had been in class and his odd behavior during the discussion of an ideal family. However, Mary attributed the minor problem they had in class to the fact that Ron was sick and simply didn't feel well enough to participate. She was still debating whether or not she should discuss the issue with someone else.

One week later Janine returned to Mary's classroom, but this time with a transfer slip. Janine had been enrolled in the eighth-grade honors class and was failing, so she was being placed in Mary's advanced class. For two weeks Mary took extra time to ensure that Janine was feeling comfortable in her new environment. She would make a point to talk with Janine for a few minutes before each class and always offer to meet with her at lunch if she needed any help. Though Janine was having no trouble academically, she frequently came in at lunch to speak with Mary. Janine was always asking Mary, "Mrs. A, are you going to the game tonight?" or "Come on, Mrs. A, please chaperone the dance. Then I can sit and talk to you." And that is exactly what Janine would do. She would stay with Mary throughout the entire event. At one game, Mary asked Janine about her parents and whether or not they were coming to see her brother play. Janine put her head down and said, "Oh, my parents are pretty old; they usually don't come." Janine appeared bothered by something, but Mary didn't feel she knew her well enough to pry when it came to family matters.

Mary, who was becoming more concerned with Janine's odd behavior, especially since she sensed the same feelings from Ron, went to see her previous English teacher. Mr. Galbraith simply stated, "Oh, there's nothing wrong with Janine. She's a bright girl; she just wasn't bright enough to be in my honors class. She's probably just feeling bad about being removed from that class." Mary asked Mr. Galbraith if he was aware of any family problems, or if possibly Janine would be having any problems with any of the other students. Again, Mr. Galbraith reassured Mary that Janine was fine. "Mary, stop worrying so much. Janine is a lovely, charming young lady. She will be fine; she just needs time to adjust." After their conversation, Mary decided to wait until the end of the week to see if there would be a change in Janine's behavior. She wasn't sure what her next move would be, but she felt if things did not improve, she would have to do something.

Two days later Mary was preparing her eighth-grade class to read "The Needle" by Isaac Bashevis Singer, a story about marriage, customs, and selecting the ideal spouse. Mary's grandparents were from Italy and products of a prearranged marriage. Mary thought this personal story would be an excellent introduction to the day's activities. Again, Mary felt this class discussion would be another avenue leading toward cultural diversity and acceptance. After sharing her grandparents' story with her students, Mary asked them to write down characteristics which their parents might consider if they were prearranging a marriage for them. They were also asked to make another list consisting of characteristics they themselves would consider in a future spouse.

As was the protocol for Mary's prereading activities, she began circulating, reading the students' responses and sharing comments and words of encouragement with them. As she came to Janine's desk, she noticed Janine was working very hard on what appeared to be an essay and not just a list of characteristics. Usually, for these prereading activities the students didn't concentrate on structure, just ideas. Mary paused at Janine's desk, and Janine handed her the paper, asking her to read it. The essay began by responding to the question Mary had asked. Janine's paper began, "I am really not sure which characteristics my parents would consider if they were choosing my ideal mate, but I hope he would be very different from my father, who, I should explain, is really my grandfather." At that point, the essay became confusing and quite disturbing. In the essay, Janine went into more detail about her difficult family situation. "You see, my grandfather is legally my father because my biological mother who is white is not permitted to raise me because my real father (who is now legally my brother) is black. My real mother's parents were so upset that they forbid her from seeing me and made her give me up when I was just a baby. Because that makes my parents, well, really my grandparents mad, they will not let me tell anyone the truth. I am supposed to tell everyone that my grandparents are actually my biological parents, and I'm not allowed to tell anyone I'm part white." At that point Mary was frozen; she didn't know what to say to Janine and was afraid to continue reading the essay which did become even more complex and upsetting. The essay concluded with, "I am being sexually abused by my grandfather, and I don't know what to do." Mary set the paper back on the desk and looked at the child who by now was sobbing hysterically. There were 28 other students in the class but one who needed Mary's undivided attention—immediately.

QUESTIONS TO CONSIDER

1. Think about the ideas being presented in the short stories Mary has chosen to present to her class. Can you think of a better way to approach this lesson? Can you think of any stories that would be more appropriate?

2. Design a prereading activity to introduce the students to the theme of marriage with respect to different cultures.

3. Is this an appropriate lesson to be teaching to students of this age?

4. When Mary sensed that there was something wrong with both Ron and Janine, should she have acted at that time?

5. What were Mary's options at that time? To whom should Mary have turned?

6. Once Mary has read Janine's paper, what should she do? What should be her first move?

7. What are the most immediate concerns that should be addressed?

8. If Mary addresses Janine's problem immediately, what should she do with the other students? What is her responsibility to them?

9. What exactly are Mary's legal responsibilities to Janine?

RECOMMENDED READINGS

Banks, J. (1988). *Multiethnic education.* Boston, MA: Allyn & Bacon.

This is a valuable book, which not only describes multiethnic education, but also offers suggestions as to how a teacher can incorporate it into the classroom.

Hidalgo, N. M., McDowell, C. L., & Siddle, V. (eds.). (1990). *Facing racism in education.* Cambridge, MA: Harvard Educational Review.

This book presents articles representing those in our society who have historically been the targets of racism. It allows the teacher to see how blind many of us have been and still are concerning the issue of racism in education.

Miller, S. (1992). *Creating change: Towards a dialogic pedagogy.* A report for the National Research Center on Literature, Teaching and Learning. Albany, NY: SUNY.

This report talks about how a teacher can create an environment of cultural acceptance through the use of classroom discussion.

Munro, A. (1987). Forgiveness in families. In Miller, McDonnell, & Hogan (eds.), *Traditions in literature.* Glenview, IL: Scott, Foresman.

This is a short story which talks about the love between the members in a family and how it can overcome trials and tribulations.

Singer, L. (1987). The needle. In Miller, McDonnell, & Hogan (eds.), *Traditions in literature.* Glenview, IL: Scott, Foresman.

This is another short story which takes a look at families. This one, however, takes a look at an old custom—prearranged marriages.

Small, R. C., Jr., & Strzepek, J. E. (1988). *A casebook for English teachers: Dilemmas and decisions.* Belmont, CA: Wadsworth.

This book provides the English teacher with specific cases of problems that teachers may experience in actual classroom settings.

THE TESTED TEACHER

GERALD P. SPECKHARD

ABSTRACT

Sally Jones discovers that test papers have been taken either in fun or as a challenge in her eighth-grade social studies class. This presents a disruption for her planned class activity as well as a challenge to her authority, especially in that most students seem to know what is going on. Will her use of peer relationships, class goodwill, teacher authority, or punishment threats help solve the classroom management problem or exacerbate it?

The Tested Teacher

Sally Jones was delighted that she had been able to land a social studies job at Oliver Ward Middle School. Social studies jobs were hard to find, especially in a good suburban school like Oliver Ward. While racially mixed (she guessed about 15 percent minority, mostly African-American), there seemed to be little tension along social, racial, or ethnic lines. Students got along fine; some of the African-Americans and a few Hispanics were social leaders, especially among boys where athletic ability had high status. Sally liked this school and wanted to do well, particularly since there were so many good social studies teachers out there ready to take her place should her first year be less than successful.

It was Monday in late September during the fourth week of school. Ms. Jones, as she was known to her students, was returning to her room after getting a drink of water between classes. She was about to meet with her eighth-grade social studies class. She had spent a large part of the weekend grading the first test of the year given to the class on Friday. She planned to return and discuss the tests during this period.

Sally Jones felt that she had gotten off to a good start, particularly with this class. The students were generally cooperative and seemed interested in their work. She was not sure, however, of her relationship with a group of boys that generally sat in the back of the room near the windows, especially several of the African-American students who seemed to be the group leaders. But she thought she had been winning them over lately.

She entered the room and went to her desk to get her gradebook to take the roll. The class, normally an easy one to get started, seemed unusually quiet. As she checked the roll, she thought to herself that perhaps the students were apprehensive about their test scores, since it was the first test of the year.

She smiled to herself, and to the class indirectly, as she reviewed in her mind the plan for the day. The class had not done as well as she had hoped on the test; she planned to go over the test in detail with pointers on how students, especially that group in the back, should organize their thinking in writing answers to the essay questions. She wasn't sure, however, how to deal with the fact that several of the African-American students had been among the lowest scorers.

After taking the roll, she gave a brief overview of the strengths and weaknesses disclosed by the test. "Now," she said, "I'll return the tests to you, and we'll go over specific questions." It was then that she noticed that the tests were not on the table beside her desk!

She was sure she had left them there. But, then again, maybe she had placed them in a drawer. As she looked through the drawers in her desk, she overheard some suppressed giggling coming from the back of the room. It dawned on her that the tests were not to be found in her desk. Someone had taken them!

As she looked up quickly, the expressions on the students' faces confirmed her suspicions. Not only was she now sure that someone in the room had taken the tests, she was also pretty sure that most of the class knew about it. Not all the members seemed in sympathy with the culprit, however; many indicated by the way they avoided looking at her and by their expressions that they disapproved of what was going on.

Was this a joke, a prank, or a challenge? Sally Jones quickly tried to assess the motive of the unknown culprit or culprits to determine her next step. She thought it might have been done in fun, but the uneasiness of many of the students indicated that it possibly had been meant as a challenge. She decided to treat it as though it were a friendly prank.

"All right, you've had your fun. Now let's get back to work. Whoever has the tests, please bring them up here." Sally Jones smiled at the class. A few students smiled back encouragingly but no one moved.

As she waited, she tried to figure out where the tests might be hidden. It was hopeless; they could be in any number of notebooks or book bags or hidden in any number of places in the room. She also thought it would be embarrassing if she made any search for them, even an indirect one.

"I should think that all of you would be interested in how you did on the test," she continued. The expressions on the faces of the students varied. Some showed embarrassment, others concern, and still others innocence. Some of the latter seemed also to reflect mockery, but could she be sure? Should she take a guess and single out one of the boys in the back? How would it be interpreted if she confronted one of the African-American students, especially if it turned out he was innocent? Perhaps if she asked one of them, she might get a clue to what was going on. She decided against it. It could backfire and show her helplessness as readily as it might produce the papers.

She felt her face flush as she tried to think of what she might try now. She realized that if the objective of the culprits was to antagonize her, they had succeeded. She also felt she had to act quickly and decisively. So she said in a firm, even voice, "I guess we'll just have to get Mr. Smith (the principal) up here to get this straightened out!" She went to the intercom and buzzed the office. When the office answered, she asked if Mr. Smith could come to her room for a moment.

She turned to the students in hopes that her action might have changed the mind of whoever had taken the tests. Most of the students were looking down at their desks or staring out of the windows. She wasn't sure she still had the sympathy of most of the students, and she felt uneasy about the possibility that her course of action might have been too drastic. She tried to explain to the class that fun was fun, but that actions by a student or students that prevented the class from getting on with its work had to be dealt with firmly. But still no one came forward with the tests or volunteered any information.

When Mr. Smith knocked on the door, she went out into the hall to explain the situation to him. Mr. Smith became quite angry and strode into the classroom. As he started to speak, Sally Jones noticed that the tests were back on her desk! She interrupted him to point out to him that the tests had been returned. He hesitated; then he turned to the class and said, "This is still a very serious matter, not only for those who took the tests but also for all of you who knew about it but didn't come forward. I want to see the entire class in here after school."

After he left, Sally Jones distributed the tests and started the discussion but it didn't go very well. Most of the students seemed uninterested and withdrawn.

While eating lunch after class, Sally Jones wondered if she had done the correct thing. Was there some other approach she should have tried? Perhaps she should talk to the principal and offer to handle the class after school herself. But even then, she wasn't sure what she should say or do to the students.

QUESTIONS TO CONSIDER

1. Would you have handled the incident in the same manner? What would you have done differently? Did any of her actions serve to exacerbate the problem?

2. Should she have searched the room either seriously or in a joking manner? Should she have prevailed more on the sympathetic students to help her to get the tests back? Could she have tried leaving the room under some pretense before calling the principal to see whether the tests would be returned, perhaps indicating that she would like the class to talk it over?

3. Assuming that you might have summoned the principal as she did, what would you do now? Did she help dig the hole she now seemed to be in?

4. Assuming that the principal "lectures" the class for a few minutes and lets them go, what should be her approach in that class the next day?

5. Should she attempt to find out who the guilty party was, directly or indirectly? What should she do if she finds out who did it? Should she act differently if the guilty party or parties were minority members?

RECOMMENDED READINGS

Charles, C. M. (1989). *Building classroom discipline,* (3rd ed.). White Plains, NY: Longman.

    Charles gives excellent summaries of eight models of discipline followed by his approach to building a personal system of discipline.

Curwin, R. L., & Mendler, A. N. (1988). *Discipline with dignity.* Washington, DC: ASCD.

Provides a well-constructed eclectic approach to classroom management emphasizing approaches that lead to self-discipline.

Emmer, E. T., Evertson, C. M., Sanford, J. P., Clements, B. S., & Worksham, M. E. (1989). *Classroom management for secondary teachers,* (2nd ed.). Englewood Cliffs, NJ: Prentice-Hall.

This excellent paperback focuses on discipline at the secondary level. Chapter 10, "Evaluating Your Classroom Organization and Management," is particularly applicable to case study analyses.

NEW TEACHER ON THE BLOCK

JACQUELINE A. STEFKOVICH
AND
MICHAEL L. SILVERMAN

ABSTRACT

John Barnes is a new teacher in Lyle, an inner-city middle school. At age 23, John has accepted this position because there was no work for him in his hometown of Appleton, a quiet, mostly white, college town. From the beginning, John experienced difficulties adjusting to the urban environment and the workings of an inner-city school. He resolved some of these issues by living outside the city with his wife, Meg, and by visiting his family and friends in Appleton on weekends. In addition, John worked hard to overcome his poor classroom evaluations. With the assistance of a supportive principal, he had begun to show improvement.

Now, just as he was beginning to adjust, John was faced with a new crisis in the form of Billy Klazinski, a strapping 165-pound streetwise kid who constantly tested John's authority. Billy was one of only three white students in the predominantly black middle school. Sent to Lyle as a disciplinary transfer, Billy had one last chance for an education in the public schools. The situation with Billy became so tense that by the end of the case study John is seriously considering quitting his job and possibly abandoning his teaching career.

New Teacher on the Block

John Barnes sat at his old beaten-up wooden desk tapping his fingers anxiously against the fake walnut finish and gazing out the window at the graffiti-covered, boarded-up buildings which constituted the Lyle Middle School neighborhood.

John was a small, thin man with delicate features, nice-looking in a wholesome Jimmy Stewart way, but hardly a Sylvester Stallone type. Right now he probably wished he were the latter. John felt as if he had the weight of the world on his shoulders. John Barnes had a serious problem and one that he needed to resolve soon.

John was young, 23, and new at this teaching game. But he'd been around or so he thought. He had done a stint in the National Guard after graduating from college and been involved in transporting supplies for Project Desert Shield. After dodging bombs in a war zone, he figured he was prepared for anything. That was before he met the kids, or more accurately one kid, at Lyle Middle School.

Now he found that he might be forced to make a choice between his career and the future of a kid he was not even sure he liked.

Commitment, But to What?

Two years ago, when John started his job in the city, it had been like coming to a different world. He was from "upstate," a rural area with rolling hills and farms and small towns. His parents' home, the place where John grew up, was in Appleton, known for its famous apple orchards and site of the local state college he had attended. Early on, John's parents, with three small children, had been too poor to go to college. Later, they were too busy building up their hardware business.

But Mr. and Mrs. Barnes valued education, and John often thought that both of them had regretted starting a family so young and, consequently, foregoing their opportunities for higher education. At any rate, there was a clear message that the Barnes' wanted more for their son, and John agreed. For as long as he could remember, John had wanted to be a teacher, and his parents, and then later his wife, Meg, encouraged him in this line of work.

John saw himself as a Mr. Chips. He loved kids, especially young children. He had been a good student who enjoyed learning new things. How wonderful it would be to impart this knowledge, to shape young minds, and see them grow.

Despite warnings from professors and classmates about the discipline problems experienced by new teachers, John was eager to teach.

He had emerged relatively unscathed from his student teaching at Appleton Elementary School. Moreover, he believed that hard work, dedication, and self-discipline would compensate for any difficulties that might arise. These qualities had always served John well before. John saw teaching as a challenge and as a lifelong career. He could not wait to begin.

In spite of his optimistic attitude, John's career began with a series of disappointments. The first came when he could not find a job in Appleton. John hadn't expected to come to the city. He thought he and Meg would spend their whole life in Appleton, raising kids, growing apples, and teaching in the local elementary school. That was his fantasy.

Evidently, others in Appleton shared John's dream. Over a hundred candidates besides John had applied for the two available positions at Appleton Elementary. John also had no better luck at schools in the surrounding towns. There were few openings, and available positions were hotly contested.

After a lengthy job search, John realized that if he really wanted to teach, he would have to go to the city. With their urban blight and serious problems, the city's schools were the only places with vacancies. To make matters worse, once John took the citywide teachers' exam and was eligible to work there, he soon discovered that he had no choice as to either the school or the grade level to which he would be assigned.

John was licensed as an elementary teacher, but in the city, "elementary" meant grades K–8. Even though the city had established middle schools, there were no special requirements to teach at these schools. Moreover, many of the people with elementary credentials preferred the earlier grades where there were fewer discipline problems and more cooperation from parents. Consequently, the middle schools generally had two kinds of employees—those sincerely dedicated to teaching and learning in the middle grades and those who got dumped there while colleagues with more seniority got their pick of schools.

John accepted his first teaching assignment at Lyle, a middle school housing 600 students, grades 6–8, and situated in one of the city's poorest neighborhoods.

John was a shy man, an introvert by most people's standards, but he was also analytical, and he tried hard to solve his problems by himself in a logical, rational manner. For instance, he hated the idea of coming to the city, so he made a compromise. He would work in the city but live an hour away in a rural-suburban setting where Meg was able to find some part-time work while she finished her degree in teaching. With this arrangement, they were also an hour closer to Appleton and could still make the three-hour trip back each weekend to visit with friends and family.

John was not fond of the city, but he had learned to survive, to make peace with this environment that had been thrust upon him. Now as he sat in his empty classroom and gazed out at what looked to him more like a bombed-out war zone than a neighborhood, he felt isolated and even a bit homesick.

Maybe things would have been different for John if he had had more control over his own fate, but it just was not meant to be. He felt powerless and frustrated. And now he felt stuck—stuck in a city he disliked, in a school that felt alien to him, teaching a grade level that he had not wanted to teach.

New Teacher Blues: Learning to Manage the Classroom

Ninety percent of the students at Lyle Middle School were African-American. The remainder were Hispanic except for three white boys, all of whom had been disciplinary transfers. Despite the fact that many of the students came from poor—and sometimes troubled—families, Lyle had a good reputation, mostly because of the leadership of its principal, Mr. Parker.

It was John's second year as a social studies teacher at Lyle. His first year had been a total disaster, and now, as early as Halloween, Mr. Parker had already evaluated him twice. The first evaluation was poor. Usually when teachers are written up, they are given two or three key areas for improvement on which they should concentrate. John was given eleven, ranging from issues of course content and teaching style to what John considered the most difficult to address—classroom management.

To make matters worse, if John got two unsatisfactory evaluations during a single academic year, he would be placed on probation. Having barely scraped through the first year, John could not afford to have problems this year. With a bad record in two consecutive years, tenure after his third year would be highly unlikely.

If Mr. Parker had not been so kind and supportive, John would have been convinced that he held some kind of vendetta against him. On the contrary, over the last few months, Mr. Parker, always on his own initiative, had spent hours discussing John's classroom problems and giving him pointers on how to improve his teaching. Much to John's amazement, some of this advice had even worked.

Mr. Parker had once told Ms. Winston, one of John's colleagues and probably his only confidante at Lyle, that John reminded him of himself twenty years ago, a young idealistic teacher from upstate, leaving everything to come to the big city. Ms. Winston's sharing of that story with John gave him at least some comfort because, even though John would not dare admit it to Ms. Winston, to himself or to anybody, he was a bit fearful of Mr. Parker. He was not sure what it was. Maybe it was his bulky frame or maybe simply because he was the principal.

John thought back to his own school days. He had gone to a junior high school rather than a middle school, and the philosophy there had been dramatically different from that of Lyle. In John's experience, the middle grades had been to prepare students for the big league, high school. There was none of this talk about school climate, cooperative planning, or teaching students as individuals. There was little emphasis upon counseling or special advising and no mention of the unique needs that kids might have at this age.

Moreover, unlike many of the boys in John's class, John did not get into a lot of trouble as a kid. He could only recall one incident, that fight with Joey King over something so insignificant that he could not remember it now. But he did remember the consternation it caused. He had never seen his usually mild-mannered father so upset. Getting sent to the principal's office was the worst. John shuddered to think of it.

Now those old childhood insecurities crept up on John as he sat in Mr. Parker's cluttered, sparsely furnished office, waiting for the results of his second evaluation. He glared at the colorful posters on the wall, not having the slightest idea what they said.

"How are you doing today?" Mr. Parker, a tall man in his late forties, asked as he stepped into the office and quietly closed the door behind him.

"OK," John said, managing to scrape up some facsimile of a smile. "Much better after we get this thing over with," he thought to himself, not daring to betray his feelings of intrepidation and then adding, silently, "Don't show weakness." Calm under stress. That is what the service had taught him.

"I take it that you still don't want a union representative to attend these meetings. You know you have that right?"

"Yes, I know. I don't think it's necessary."

The first time Mr. Parker had asked John this question, at his first evaluation last year, John had felt threatened. Was something going to be said that necessitated union intervention?

By now, John realized that the question was pro forma. He didn't even think about it, or the answer, anymore. He didn't believe in unions. While he would never tell anyone at the school, he really thought teachers' unions existed to shield weak people, those who were looking for an easy way out and wanted to be protected. He didn't think he needed that kind of help. He could handle this on his own.

Mercifully, Mr. Parker got to the point quickly, almost as soon as he sat in the old, overstuffed swivel-chair, its simulated leather buckling under the strain of his weight.

"What did you think about the lesson today? What did you see as your strengths and weaknesses?" Mr. Parker was talking about John's fourth-period class which he had observed that morning.

"I think I've improved, but it still wasn't great," John began tentatively. He knew this would be Mr. Parker's first question. It always was. He thought he would be prepared for it, but he felt himself crumbling as he blurted out, "The kids aren't responding to my management system." Then he paused, looked down at the dusty wooden floor, and shook his head slowly, realizing that he had blown it. "I don't know. Maybe I'll never get it," he said to himself.

"I also see some improvement, John," Mr. Parker began. "A lot of improvement. Your teaching methods are much better, and I think you have developed a good rapport with the students in your classes."

John caught his breath, hoping his sigh of relief was not too obvious. It was true. He had improved. He had worked hard to improve. "Maybe everything's OK, after all. I did do a good job. I deserve some recognition," he thought to himself. But his feelings of relief and satisfaction were short-lived.

"I also agree with you regarding your classroom management. Your class was better today than before, but you still have a long way to go. Here is a list of things that should help you." Mr. Parker handed John the list of a dozen or so items. John skimmed it quickly, seeing recommendations such as, "Don't talk over the children. Circulate around the room as you're teaching. Project your voice."

They reviewed the list item by item. One suggestion particularly stuck in John's mind. "Raising your voice doesn't make children listen, John. Try to make your voice sound deeper and more assertive. Try to project your voice, rather than just making it louder."

John was taken aback by this advice and felt a little offended. After all, this person was telling him how to talk, perhaps even how to talk like a man, that is, with a deep voice. On the other hand, he had to admit that Mr. Parker was probably right. It would be a hard habit to break.

After they were done with the list, Mr. Parker said in a kind, but firm, manner, "John, I am going to give you a satisfactory rating this time around. But it's a *marginal* satisfactory rating. It will go on your record as a satisfactory, but I want you to know—just between us—that I am still concerned about your classroom management. If you cannot improve on these areas by your next evaluation, I will be forced to give you another unsatisfactory."

John was relieved to get a satisfactory rating, even under these conditions. "If he only knew the half of it," John said to himself, thinking about Billy Klazinski, the new addition to his classroom. It was a good thing Mr. Parker's observation had been during the fourth period instead of the third.

After what seemed like an interminable pause, Mr. Parker stood up, smiled at John and said, "Listen, I really do want to help you. If there is *anything* I can do, please stop down and talk to me about it."

John hesitated for a moment, as if he were pondering some proposition. "No way," he thought to himself. As decent as Mr. Parker may be, he is still the principal, and the last thing he needs to hear about is the saga of Billy Klazinski. It would be like opening Pandora's box.

"Take the satisfactory and run," John said to himself, deciding that he had a few months to get out of this dilemma. He was pretty sure that he could improve on many of the areas Mr. Parker had suggested. He was not so sure he could do anything about Billy, his major discipline problem. Sometime before his next evaluation, he would figure out some way to deal with Billy Klazinski.

John thought about Billy, the source of many of his problems, and had no idea as to what could be done with this kid. He was a punk, a real troublemaker, and to make matters worse, he was disrupting a class that John had spent months trying to get into shape. John was not sure what to do next, but he was sure that he had to get a plan—and soon.

Teacher Survival: Learning a New Set of Rules

There were days when John felt as if some alien spaceship had picked him up and set him down in a strange, hostile world. His idea of what teaching would be like and the reality of teaching were so far apart that he wondered if he had not been living in some fantasy world.

Despite the fact that there was a college in town, the population of Appleton was amazingly homogeneous. There were the "townies," the townsfolk who ran small businesses and waited patiently for the college students to leave. Then there were the students themselves, mostly first-generation college graduates like himself from similar, middle-class backgrounds. No matter how intellectually broadening college might have been and how good the teacher-education program was, it had hardly prepared John for what he encountered at Lyle.

As John drove through the neighborhood to work, he saw drug pushers, fourteen-year-old prostitutes, and dirt. Dirt was everywhere! He simply did not understand how people could live this way. There was a crackhouse across the street from the school and middle-school children who had no idea who their fathers were. There were children having children. Sure, there were poor people back home, but those people lived on farms and went to church and folks in the community helped them out. Urban poverty seemed so different; it was beyond John's comprehension.

John attended one of the district's induction meetings for a grueling four hours after school one night a month. Most teachers thought the experience was totally worthless, and John was no exception. But it was required for new teachers, so John forced himself to attend. He sat in the back for a quick getaway. The person seated next to him was a tall, well-dressed, African-American man about John's age.

"Hi. I'm Brad Johnson," the man began with a friendly smile. This was the beginning of a long discussion about the woes of new teachers.

It turned out that Brad and John had much in common. They were both in their second year of teaching. Their schools were in the same section of the city. And, by an odd coincidence, or a good stroke of luck, they had grown up in neighboring towns. Brad Johnson came from a middle-class African-American family and had graduated from a well-known small, private college near Appleton. John was impressed. The school had a fine reputation.

"I have many of the same problems you have," said Brad. "It's difficult to discipline kids, and these city kids are different. I think they don't respect me because I'm not as streetwise as they are. I just never had to be."

Brad and John talked about the pace of the city, how hard it was to keep up, and how neither of their wives were happy with the move. But there was one fundamental difference.

"Despite it all, I like the city," Brad said. "There's so much to do, so many cultural things. I like living here so that I can be near it all."

During the course of the conversation, John learned much about the city. Brad had evidently made a study of the place, trying to find out as much about urban life as he could. In addition, he was very involved with the parents in the school.

"There are lots of people in the neighborhood who want the same thing for their kids that you and I want. And they're working hard to get it. But you don't see those people on the news. Nobody is interested in them. They're prisoners in their own homes, trying to manage in the neighborhood. Most of those people have nothing to do with the drugs. They can't afford them. It's a few neighborhood pushers. The clientele are yuppies from the suburbs—doctors, lawyers, businessmen. Can you believe it? It's really pathetic. No wonder the neighborhood people get so discouraged."

Brad was exuberant and John mesmerized. In his disgust for the city, John had never thought about these things, certainly not how middle-class people might have worsened the situation. And do you know why there are so many vacant lots in the neighborhood?" Brad continued.

"No," John shook his head.

"It's because City University bought up all this property, had the buildings condemned, tore them down, and then ran out of money to put anything in their place. Some social responsibility, huh?"

John had to agree. It seemed like a dumb thing for the university to do. No wonder the people in the neighborhood thought so little of City U.

It had been an interesting evening for John. He couldn't say that he felt the sympathy for the neighborhood people that Brad did, and certainly he liked the city no better. But the conversation helped him to understand the situation a little better and to see, from another perspective, the problems his students faced. John was also grateful to meet someone from home, someone who had experienced some of the same problems he had and someone with whom he felt comfortable enough to talk. Teaching at Lyle had been an isolating experience. John was grateful for the support Brad had offered.

It was ironic that now, just when things were looking up, when John had made peace with the city, when he had started to understand the rules in this school and in the community, when his classes were finally starting to get under control, along came Billy Klazinski. John felt like Sisyphus, the mythological figure who kept lugging that big rock up the hill only to have it pull him back down again when he was almost to the top.

Billy: Oppressor or Oppressed?

Billy Klazinski was the biggest sixth grader that John had ever seen. He wasn't just tall. He was BIG. With a large neck and broad shoulders, he must have weighed at least 165 pounds. He had brown eyes, sandy blond hair, and pale skin that bespoke his Eastern European heritage.

In an attempt to explain Billy's behavior, Lyle's Dean of Discipline had once told John that Billy "lived on the dark side." John did not quite understand what the Dean meant by this. The concept became clearer as John began reading Billy's records.

Billy was what the city schools called a "disciplinary transfer." This classification put it mildly to say the least. Lyle was the third school Billy had attended in the last three years. There were no other middle schools left in this particular district, and Central Office had a policy against cross-district transfers. So, essentially, Lyle was Billy's last hope or, less optimistically, a holding ground until he finally dropped out of school or ended up in a juvenile detention center.

In addition, Billy had been suspended twice already this year, and the Dean of Discipline was reluctant to suspend him again, as it would mean having to submit a report to the central office and deal with ensuing grief, endless explanations, and bureaucracy.

Billy's academic records were not much better than his disciplinary history. He had failed two grades already. He was 14 years old and this was his second time in sixth grade. Despite an average IQ (full scale score of 107), his grades were mostly D's. The biggest deviations were the "F" that Billy had received in John's class and a "B" in science from Ms. Winston.

A note in Billy's folder said that he had been referred for special education services but that he was not eligible. He had had a complete workup from the school psychologist who had said that he might have a slight learning disability, but nothing serious enough to merit remediation.

Moreover, Billy's history of discipline problems did not make him eligible for services. He was described as having a conduct disorder, which means that he had a history of misbehavior even in grade school but no emotional problems.

Flipping through the discipline case reports, John recognized those on top. They were from him.

Monday, November 1:

Billy was throwing a football in class. He was asked to give the football up. Billy refused. After I began to write a discipline referral, Billy took it off my desk. He continued to toss the football up in the air throughout class.

Wednesday, November 3:

Billy was running around the room. He was chasing after Doren Harris.

Tuesday, November 16:

Billy was sitting in the closet after he was told to sit in the classroom.

When he finally did come out, he disrupted the class. He also disrupted the class on November 15 by talking out and walking around the classroom.

Wednesday, November 17:

Billy was out of his seat when he and Kira Lopez started fighting. Billy threw a book at Kira that hit her on the face. [Billy was suspended for three days after this incident.]

Tuesday, November 25:

During class today, Billy did the following: Talking during class, asked if he could get a drink of water, was told no. Billy then walked out of class and went to the fountain. Billy returned to class. Another student was returning to the room. Billy met him at the door and pushed him in the hall. Billy followed the student out into the hall and was pushing him and wrestling with the student. The teacher asked Billy at least twice to return to the room. Billy came in. He was still out of his seat and talking. Billy was told to leave. He moved at me as if he wanted to fight. Again, he was told to leave. He left the classroom and hung outside the room, banging on the door.

As John reviewed the records, he found that other teachers had similar problems with Billy. Billy would curse at the women teachers using epithets such as "Leave me the F_ _ _ alone" and "Don't you touch me, B_ _ _ _ "and would taunt them by getting into their "personal space" and speaking to them with a cold, menacing smile on his face. Often, he never said anything threatening, just made them feel very uneasy.

Most of Billy's teachers were female, and he happily intimidated them. He also took great joy in making John feel like less of a man.

John had hoped that special education was the answer. With that possibility eliminated, he was left wondering what to do next. He felt that Billy was like a keg of dynamite waiting to explode, and he silently prayed that the explosion would not happen in his class.

With a Little Help From My Friends

John was vulnerable. He was losing weight and not sleeping and his nerves were on edge. It was obvious that the situation was getting worse, and he wasn't sure with whom he could talk. Eventually, he realized that he would have to discuss this with one of the administrators, perhaps Mr. Parker. But not yet. Not now. He had to somehow fix this himself. But he needed advice from someone with whom he felt comfortable, from someone in whom he could confide.

Hazel Winston, science teacher for the fifth and sixth grades, was probably the best-liked and most respected teacher at Lyle Middle

School. She had been teacher of the year the previous year. She was a slender, elegant-looking, African-American woman in her early sixties but with the vibrance and enthusiasm generally associated with much younger teachers.

"I'm having problems with a student in my third-period class," John began, hesitantly, wondering how much he really wanted to divulge about "the Billy situation."

"Oh?" Ms. Winston began. "What can I do to help?"

"I'm not sure," John said. "I guess I could use some advice."

"Why not?" she said. "Tell me the problem."

John was encouraged by her receptivity and began to relax as he told his story.

"There's this student in my third-period class. He gives me a lot of trouble, and he's failing social studies. So I went through his records a few days ago and found out that he gives a lot of his teachers a hard time and his grades are terrible, even though he's fairly bright. But the one thing that I did notice was that he has a "B" in science and there were no discipline referrals from you in his file. So, I wondered why he does so well in your class and what you do that's different from my approach.

"Sounds like Billy Klazinski."

"That's the kid."

"Billy, what do I do with Billy?" she said, deep in thought, pressing her index finger into her cheek.

"Well, for one thing, I talked to him early on. I didn't let it get too far along. I could tell that he wasn't taking the work seriously. He wasn't paying attention. He would fidget, doodle while I was talking, squirm around in his seat. Then he failed his first quiz. So I had him stay after class, and I said to him, 'Billy, none of the children I've taught have been stupid. You don't want to be the first in forty years, do you?' That was that. After our 'little talk,' Billy did really well in science. I even think he began to enjoy the class. He seems to have a real aptitude for it—science, that is.

Don't misunderstand me. He's not the perfect student. He still has some lapses. But overall, he does pretty well. Every opportunity I get, I try to react to how smart he is rather than to how bad he is."

Ms. Winston continued, giving John a few more pointers on how to motivate kids like Billy. After a while, despite having received what he was certain was good advice from Ms. Winston, he still wasn't sure that he had heard the answer for which he was looking.

"Yes, but what do you do about disciplinary problems?" he managed to eke out, hoping that he had disguised any sounds of desperateness in his voice. "Why is it that Billy never seems to give you a hard time?" John asked.

"Well," she paused, thinking, then continued. "He tries. . . . I just don't let him get away with it."

"So, what do you do?"

She paused again and then said, "Here's an example. Have you noticed how Billy has that annoying habit of getting up in people's faces when he talks to them?"

"Ha! The understatement of the year," John thought, but just nodded tentatively, wondering where Ms. Winston was going with this point.

"He tried that with me once," she continued. "But he doesn't do it any more. I put him in his place. I beat him to the punch. Even if he looks like he's headed that way, I do it to him first. And, you know," she said wisely, shaking her head. "He doesn't like someone doing it to him any more than the rest of us do."

"But, what do you do when he really gets out of control?"

"It's a secret," she said. "But I guess I could tell you if it would help. Just don't go around talking about it."

Considering John's naturally introverted personality and his sense of isolation in the school, this warning was hardly necessary, but it flattered John that Ms. Winston chose to divulge her secrets to him, and flattered him still more that she actually thought that he might have someone to tell. The secrecy also seemed to add a sense of mystery and heightened importance to the forthcoming advice. John waited intently.

"Sometimes when he's really acting up, like that crazy stuff he does in the hall, running around, banging on doors . . . .Sometimes when he does that, I'll take him into my room and I'll speak to him, and maybe even hug him, until he's calm."

John tried to picture the incongruity of this scene—Ms. Winston, an articulate, exquisitely dressed, aristocratic-looking, gentle black woman with her arms around this big hulk of a white kid who looked like he'd come right off the streets, ripped jeans, studded jacket, and all. The whole idea of it boggled John's mind. Ms. Winston's voice jolted him back to reality.

"Billy's big," she continued. "He's a big kid. But he's still a kid. He's young and he needs support and he can't get much at home."

It was then that John found out about Billy's home life.

"Billy is the youngest of three children. His brother, Keith, is eighteen and unemployed. He dropped out of school early on and has been in and out of jail for a variety of things—vandalism, stealing, assault. He's a real street fighter, that one, really bad news." She continued with a sigh, shaking her head. "Trouble is, Billy idolizes him."

"Some role model, huh?" she asked rhetorically and concluded. "The East End is a tough place. It's not a place to raise children."

"You said three children. What about the other one?"

"Oh, that would be Sheila. She's a ninth grader. She's a good student and stays pretty much out of trouble. Except that she's pregnant."

"Pregnant?"

"It happens," Ms. Winston said kindly as if she were trying not to offend John's sensibilities.

"And Billy's parents. What about them?"

"The father's out of the picture. Deserted Billy's mother and the kids years ago. I doubt that Billy even remembers him."

"And the mother?"

"I don't know much about her. Just what I've heard from others around the school. She's an unemployed hairdresser. Picks up a little part-time work on the side, but my sense is that she's not too successful at it. She's got three kids, no husband, and an eighth-grade education. It can't be easy. It might be a good idea to talk to her, though. She might lend some insight into Billy's behavior and give you a better sense of where Billy is coming from."

John sighed. It was an audible sigh and one born out of frustration and anxiety. He dreaded talking with parents. He hated the whole thing. He hated making the phone call home. He hated trying to explain why the parents should come in. Most of all, he hated trying to defend his own, admittedly inept, handing of the situation to these sometimes hostile strangers.

On the other hand, he knew that communicating with parents was important, especially in situations like Billy's. It was the professional thing to do. In his heart and in his mind, John knew that Ms. Winston was right. It was his stomach that didn't favor this strategy.

Ms. Winston must have sensed John's discomfort. She put her hand on his shoulder and looked him straight in the eye.

"You know, John," she hesitated, "us teachers . . . . We're fragile, sensitive people. Gentle folk. That's why we got into teaching. The profession attracts people who care, who want to make a difference, people like us. But for that reason, it can eat us up, too. It's not always so easy bringing kids around. Teaching is not only a science, it's also an art. And creating good art takes a lot of hard work and patience . . . and practice."

Ms. Winston paused, and then added with a kind expression, "You think great paintings like this were made in a day?" She waved her arm in a dramatic flourish, pointing at the poster of Picasso's "Guernica" hanging on the classroom wall near her desk.

Despite his low mood, John had to smile at that one. He was familiar with the painting and its hodgepodge of bodies and heads that didn't quite match. Ms. Winston's analogy seemed to fit on several levels. After all, it was a painting about war.

A Clash of Culture and Values: The Meeting with Mrs. Klazinski

John did not dislike Mrs. Klazinski. It was something different from dislike. Maybe he did not respect her. Certainly, he did not understand her. She came from a culture and background so different from his that he simply could not relate to this woman. If pressed, he might say that they had different values. But if the truth were to be known, and if John were uncharitable enough to admit his true feelings (which he was not), he might say that Mrs. Klazinski simply did not have values. Certainly, her "values" were not any with which he was familiar.

Mrs. Klazinski lived on the East End. By far, one of the roughest neighborhoods in the city, the East End had previously consisted of white, blue-collar laborers who had worked in the mills. After the mills shut down, around fifteen years ago, those who could, or wanted to, left the neighborhood for better jobs. Others stayed, out of allegiance to the neighborhood or lack of ambition or other motivation.

Prostitution and drug dealing began to take the place of heavy manufacturing as the major industry. The neighborhood remained mostly white with fringes of poor African-Americans and Hispanics. Regardless of race or ethnicity, this neighborhood attracted the seediest element of the city. It was here that Mrs. Klazinski, uneducated, jobless, and abandoned by her husband, lived and raised her three children.

Mrs. Klazinski was a large woman, larger than John both in height and girth and, even though her voice was soft, she had Billy's same annoying habit of standing too close to John when she spoke. Her short blonde hair was dark at the roots and frizzy, and she wore pale blue polyester slacks with a large white over-blouse that made her look pregnant.

John felt frustrated with Billy and ill at ease with his mother as he blurted out the problem.

"Mrs. Klazinski, you have got to do something with Billy. He's totally disrupting my class. This week alone, he . . . ." John then followed up with a virtual litany of Billy's offenses ranging anywhere from running around the classroom to fighting to throwing things at other students.

"But you don't understand," Mrs. Klazinski began as she got up in John's face. "Billy has a lot of problems. I have a lot of problems. We have a hard life. There's nothing I can do. I'm struggling just to get us all fed."

As she spoke, her voice became more frantic and bitter.

"What with bus fares and all, I don't have the money to keep coming up here. And this damned school system won't put Billy back in our neighborhood school where he belongs. I don't understand all this. Billy shouldn't be here with these kids anyway. Did you know that there are only two other white kids in this school besides Billy?"

The meeting continued in this vein for a while and then finally deteriorated into a contest of wills with Mrs. Klazinski blaming the school, Billy's father, and then John for all Billy's problems and John trying to make sense of the whole thing and, with some irony, defending both the school and his classroom management strategies.

The conversation reached its lowest ebb when Mrs. Klazinski defended her son's past record of indiscretions, saying emphatically to John, "But it wasn't Billy's fault that he threw the chair at that teacher."

On this note, John ended the ninety-minute interview realizing that he was getting nowhere fast. It looked as if Billy's mother would be no help in solving either John's or Billy's problems. His best hope for the day was that Mr. Parker would not see Mrs. Klazinski leaving the building in this state.

The Final Episode

John sat on the side of his bed staring into space. A brisk winter wind rattled the window and gently stirred the white tie-back curtains as it penetrated the cracks around the storm windows. It was a dark, dismal mid-December day.

Things had gotten increasingly worse at school. Despite Ms. Winston's good advice, John had gotten nowhere with Billy and, consequently, the other students in the class had followed suit. Mrs. Klazinski had stopped coming to school and had hung up on John the last time he had tried to call her. To make matters worse, Mr. Parker had told John that he would be observing his third-period class on Monday, Billy's class.

John sat, in a daze, unable to move.

"John, are you coming?" he heard Meg's voice from the bottom of the steps.

"Yes," he mumbled, almost inaudibly, without budging. He was dressed, but he had forgotten to shave—again. The blond stubble on his chin and cheeks scratched as he stroked his face. Maybe he would try to grow a beard. Or maybe not.

Meg appeared in the doorway. She had on blue jeans and a bright red turtleneck, the uniform she wore for taking final exams. Her long brown hair was pushed back from her face and tied with a red ribbon at the nape of her neck. She was a pretty woman in a clean, natural sort of way.

Meg was not a nag. She never had been. But she was concerned, and this concern showed in her voice as she asked John for the third time that morning, "Are you coming? Are you going to work today? It's late."

Every day for the past few weeks, John had been a little later. Teachers were expected to be in their rooms 45 minutes before the start of school. Yesterday, John had barely made it in time for homeroom period.

Meg was quiet this morning as she rushed him off to work. They had had this discussion before. She had told him to quit if he wanted to, that she'd work full-time until he got something else. There was no need to rehash things now.

Once at school, John had a similar discussion with Ms. Winston. "John, look at you. Every day, you come in a little later, looking a little more scruffy. Look at what this is doing to you. You've got to pull out of it.

"John," she said, looking directly into his eyes and speaking in a kind voice. "Nothing is worth all this."

Ms. Winston left John deep in contemplation.

Somewhere along the way, John's idealism had failed him. It hadn't been enough to pull him through. Teaching was all that John had ever wanted to do. Now, as he rose slowly from his desk and headed toward Mr. Parker's office, he sensed two competing feelings—one a sense of relief as if a heavy burden had been lifted from him and the other a deep sense of loss.

QUESTIONS TO CONSIDER

1. What are the major issues presented in this case?

2. Some might see John as a good teacher in the wrong school. Do you agree or disagree? Why?

3. How much control does John have over his situation? What are the things that he can change and cannot change?

4. What steps, if any, did John take to improve his situation? Were they effective? Why or why not?

5. If you were in John's place, what would you do?

6. Do you think John's problems would have been different if he had been female or of another race or ethnicity? Explain your reasoning.

7. Do other staff in the school have a professional responsibility to help a new teacher? If so, who? How far does this responsibility, if any, extend?

8. What lessons can be learned from this case? For new teachers? For experienced teachers?

9. Do you think that John should either quit his job at Lyle Middle School or, perhaps, leave the teaching profession all together? Why or why not?

10. What do you think happens after the last scene in this case?

RECOMMENDED READINGS

Bullard, S. (1991). "Sorting Through the Multicultural Rhetoric." *Educational Leadership,* 49: 4–7.

    This article stresses that the goal of a good multicultural curriculum should be to transform the school so that all students, without exception, will experience an equal opportunity to learn. To accomplish this goal, teachers should empower students from all groups by teaching them decision-making and socialization skills. Finally, teachers should help students develop cross-cultural dependency and view themselves from the perspective of other groups.

Bullard, S. (1992). "Celebrate values: An interview with Robert Coles." *Teaching Tolerance,* 1(1): 18–23.

    Sara Bullard, editor of *Teaching Tolerance,* interviews Robert Coles, a Harvard professor and eminent child psychologist. Here, Dr. Coles describes how educators should incorporate values into the classroom. He stresses the importance of art and stories in teaching values and in facilitating a teacher's understanding of how children perceive differences.

Morris, J. (1992). "Somebody to Lean On." *Teacher,* 4: 36–37.

    In this article, John Morris discusses the need for teachers to build relationships with colleagues in school. He stresses the hardships teachers can face because they are isolated in their classrooms and the important role that collegial dialogue and support can play in helping teachers to cope with this isolation.

THE RISE AND FALL OF BRUNO REILLY: THE SUPERINTENDENT FROM HELL

JANET W. WOHLBERG

ABSTRACT

Bruno Reilly appeared determined to "whip" the Marsh County School system "into shape." Fortunately or unfortunately, depending on your point of view, not everyone agreed with Reilly's mission and/or approach to "educational reform." To achieve his ends, Reilly used threats and harassment, and introduced change by fiat. This case asks readers to consider what does and does not constitute an appropriate approach to the management of change in a school system and to look at the advantages and disadvantages of autocratic leadership in the management of a system that may be in trouble. The case also asks readers to consider what the appropriate roles of various stakeholders—principals, teachers, school boards, unions—ought to be in bringing about educational reform, and what the working relationship should be between these stakeholders and the superintendent.

The Rise and Fall of Bruno Reilly: The Superintendent from Hell

Background

The five suburbs of Marsh County fall to the east and south of a diverse and run-down city. During the decades of the seventies and eighties, the increasingly affluent population had taken to the proverbial hills, away from the row houses and apartment buildings that had been home to their parents and grandparents and to a lifestyle that included lawns, houses with attached garages, and small suburban shopping centers. Three of the five suburban neighborhoods were largely middle income and blue collar; one was dominated by second and third generation Italian-Americans; one was heavily populated by the offspring of Scandinavian farmers; and the other was a mixture that also included families descended from the Irish and Eastern Europeans who came on the various waves of immigration throughout the late nineteenth and early twentieth centuries. While the remaining two suburbs were a mix of all of the above, the communities as a whole, including Elmore Township, were far more affluent. It was in these two suburbs that the area's country clubs, private schools, and fine specialty boutiques were located.

Anyone who had enough money to get out of the city had done so, and along with the people went the businesses that had supported the growing community. Left behind were the elderly living on fixed incomes and the poor. In the late eighties, there was also an influx of immigrants from Asia, Haiti, South and Central America, and the Middle East. It was a scene that was being replicated all over the United States.

As Marsh County expanded, so did its school system. By the time Bruno Reilly arrived to take over the superintendency, the system included three high schools, one of which served the inner city, the other two drawing their students from the suburbs. There were also six middle and nine elementary schools. The separation between suburban and urban populations was well-defined. Because of the pattern of growth in the county, the suburban schools were newer and better equipped than those of the city. Grassy ballfields and extensive playgrounds contrasted sharply with the cracked concrete school yards of the city with their heavy-duty chain link surrounds. The city's only middle school, like its high school, was a dark, overcrowded place. Science classes were held in the bathrooms, the only places with running water and appropriate ventilation.

Helen Tedeschi

Helen Tedeschi had started as a teacher in the Marsh County school system shortly after graduating from college. Over her 30 years in education, she had been promoted from teacher to head teacher to assistant principal and, ultimately, to principal of Elmore Junior High, Marsh County's most prestigious middle school. She had served several terms as an elected member of the school committee and had spearheaded the introduction of drug and alcohol education and the enrichment of the county's science education programs. Prior to assuming her administrative duties at Elmore, Tedeschi also had served two terms as president of the Teachers' Alliance, the largest teacher union in the state.

Tedeschi's husband, a pediatrician, had a large private practice in addition to his work in the pediatric clinic of the county hospital. The couple lived in a seven-bedroom house with rolling lawns. Two of their three children had attended the local public schools and had gone on to Ivy League colleges. The third child was entering grade 8 at Elmore.

Considered the "principal's principal," Tedeschi was often consulted by principals from the other suburban schools in Marsh County for advice and support, particularly when problems had political overtones. Many teachers also admired her; a position at her school was considered to be the best assignment a teacher could have within the entire Marsh system, so whenever she had an opening—which was rare—applications were plentiful. In addition to liking Tedeschi, teachers found the largely white and upper-middle-class students at Elmore to be easier to teach than the more socioeconomically and racially diverse populations that existed elsewhere in the system. Tedeschi encouraged her teachers to recruit classroom aides from among their friends, giving meetings on professional days the aura of suburban ladies' lunches. The level of cooperation among the teachers was high, and they socialized widely both in and out of school.

Tedeschi set high standards. The occasional teacher who did not measure up would receive support and mentoring, but once Tedeschi concluded that it was useless, she would quietly work with the teacher to think about and find other career opportunities. It was rare for a teacher to resist Tedeschi's assistance in exploring other options: those who did generally left for one of the other schools in the system or located elsewhere.

Tedeschi encouraged her teachers to be innovative in the classroom and to share ideas with their colleagues. Each month, she gave an innovation award, and the recipient's photograph, along with a description of the innovation, was posted in a visible place in the school office.

She also instituted a resource file in the teachers' room and encouraged frequent collaboration.

Students at Tedeschi's school appeared, from all traditional measures, to be among the best prepared in Marsh County: most graduated, went on to high school and then to college. Helen Tedeschi made a point of learning the students' names, and she maintained good relationships with their parents by keeping in regular touch through meetings, telephone calls, and a monthly newsletter. A number of the parents belonged to the same country club as Tedeschi and her husband.

For Tedeschi, being a teacher and then a principal was virtually an ideal situation. While she understood teacher burnout, for her, being an educator was exhilarating. It was not until Bruno Reilly came to town that Helen Tedeschi was really touched by at least some of the problems that she had been able to avoid but that she knew existed in some places in Marsh County and in other school systems. For the most part, Reilly's predecessors had been hands-off, laissez faire managers who often couldn't even be found when problems arose. As far as Tedeschi was concerned, that was just great. She ran her school as if it were private, and as long as she stayed within her budget, she was left alone.

Bruno Reilly

Bruno Reilly, now 57 years old, had received his undergraduate education from a Midwestern university. His degree, in English literature, had led to a job teaching in a public school, a position he had held while taking courses nights and summers to earn his masters and eventually his doctorate in education. After receiving his Ed.D., Reilly accepted a position as a principal at an inner-city high school in New Jersey. Almost immediately, he became known as a reformer. Within two years, absenteeism at the school had dropped by more than 30 percent, grades on standardized tests had improved, and the number of students enrolled in the college track had increased.

Four years later, Reilly left the principal's position to become superintendent of a small school system in Ohio. Many modern teaching methods had been instituted throughout this system, but something was clearly amiss. Student scores on standardized tests were the lowest in the state, and a high percentage of even the best students dropped out before high school graduation to take low-paying, dead-end factory jobs. The local school board gave Reilly a clear mandate: "Clean this mess up, get rid of the deadwood, cut the budget, and we'll back you up with whatever you need." Thus, one of Reilly's first acts after reviewing the files of his predecessor was to call the principals together and read them the proverbial 'riot act.'

"You people," he told them, "are clearly not doing your jobs. Good students aren't graduating, virtually no one is college-bound. You and you alone bear the responsibility for what is being allowed to happen here, and I'm going to hold you to that responsibility."

Reilly then gave orders to fire several teachers whom he considered inadequate, and he told three principals that they could consider themselves to be "on probation," saying that they too would be terminated if student performance at their schools did not markedly improve.

The meeting ended with the principals filing out of Reilly's office, one by one. No one looked up.

Student performance did improve, about 15 percent of the high school's graduates began to go on to college, and the students' scores on standardized tests rose from last in the state to close to the middle. Despite this, teachers and principals, angry at Reilly's heavy-handed tactics, waged war against him. In parent-teacher conferences, in chats with their neighbors and friends, the teachers and principals expressed their feelings that Reilly was standing in the way of real progress, that he was mishandling school funds, and that any improvements were being made in spite of him, not because of him. Two principals who had been demoted by Reilly as part of a school consolidation ran for school board and won. Reilly's contract was not renewed. Five years later, performance within the system was virtually back to where it had been prior to Reilly's regime.

The stories of Reilly's subsequent jobs seemed to parallel that of his Ohio superintendency. Reilly came in, turned each system inside out, got rid of people he considered to be nonperformers, upped the standards, instituted stringent rules and regulations for principals and teachers as well as for students, and ultimately was forced out.

The Marsh County School System

Ten days after moving into his office in Marsh County, Bruno Reilly summoned the system's principals to his office. It was Friday afternoon at 4 p.m. when the group gathered. Using overhead transparencies, Reilly proceeded to give a two-hour, fully illustrated talk on the problems in the schools. With charts and graphs, Reilly explained that student scores on standardized tests had been going down all over the district, and he explained—in detail—the ten-step improvement plan that was to be undertaken. Included was the designation of a group of 'magnet' schools which were to receive additional funding in order to support enrichment programs. Elmore Middle School was not among them.

"We'll admit only the best students to the magnet schools," Reilly told the principals. "If you want good students, you're going to have to make your schools competitive."

"Otherwise," he added, "you'll just have to make do with the dregs."

Toward the end of his presentation, Reilly put an overhead on the screen that shocked everyone. In the left-hand column was a list of teachers whom Reilly had tagged for dismissal, transfer, or probation. On the right side of the graphic, Reilly had listed the names of those principals whose contracts would not be renewed or who were to be demoted. He also announced that art, music, and sports programs would be cut to the minimum required by the state and that these, along with drama and other electives, were to be replaced with mandatory, supervised study halls beginning in grade five.

"We're going to run this place like a business, and I intend to turn out students who know the basics," Reilly said. "There will be no social passes. Kids will stay in their grades until they can master the material or they're too old for school. Anyone of you who can't cut it is out."

It was vintage Reilly. "You people," he said, pointing his finger in a sweeping arc, "have been getting away with too much for too long. I intend to hold you accountable for what happens to our students. If they don't make it, neither will you. This means all of the students—no matter what their background; and it means getting some teachers and paraprofessionals into this system who can talk their language and lay down the rules. I want to start seeing some faces around these schools that look more like the students, people who can get through to these kids and understand discipline."

On Monday, Helen Tedeschi received the following memo with instructions to distribute it to every teacher and to post it in the teachers' room:

All classrooms in the Marsh County School System will henceforth return to traditional and rigorous learning modes. Desks are to be arranged in straight rows. Seating is to be alphabetical by the first letter of the last name of each student. Attendance is to be taken at the beginning and end of each class. Late or absent students are to receive a zero for the day, and parents are to be notified, in writing, within 24 hours of their child's lateness or absence. The enclosed rules of behavior are to be posted in each classroom in a prominent place in block letters a minimum of two inches high. Inspection of classrooms will take place in seven to ten days.

B. Reilly

Attached to the memo was a list of 15 rules of behavior, including prohibitions against gum chewing, slouching at desks, and talking during class time. Helen Tedeschi read through the memo and blanched. She had begun to move toward a cooperative learning approach at Elmore Middle School, and her efforts had been met with enthusiasm. Thus, she wasn't surprised when she found herself with a virtual insurrection on her hands when the memo was distributed. She knew she had to get to Reilly to tell him about the problems that were arising from this set of sudden changes, and she hoped that he would be willing to spend some time discussing other approaches.

After several calls to Reilly with no return call, Tedeschi finally succeeded in getting through. "What do you think you're doing?" she asked him. "Teachers need to be able to reach these kids in more exciting ways. We're dealing with kids who have been raised on sound bytes, and this kind of passive, traditional teaching just doesn't work anymore."

"Then send a memo to the parents to turn their televisions off," Reilly snarled. "This doesn't take genius—but then, there doesn't seem to be much of that around here."

The phone went dead.

Over the next several years, Tedeschi received edict after edict from Reilly. While she had to admit that a few of his ideas were good, she generally ignored everything that came to her from the superintendent's office. Sometimes she was able to get away with not implementing Reilly's mandated changes, but just as often, Reilly would show up at her door, unannounced, and demand to know why a change hadn't been made or a memo hadn't been posted. He was always back within a day or two to be sure that his orders had been followed; and knowing she could no longer ignore Reilly's directives without further harassment, Tedeschi had grudgingly complied. "Don't ask," she told the teachers, "just do it."

From the teachers, Tedeschi learned that Reilly would suddenly appear in the classrooms, take a seat in the front row, and grill them in the middle of a lesson about what it was they were teaching and why. Despite Tedeschi's efforts to support and reassure her faculty, teacher morale plummeted, and Tedeschi herself lost a great deal of her positive motivation. Instead, she became increasingly driven by anger and frustration, aware as she was of the painful changes at Elmore Middle School. She was no longer able to select her own teachers, nor were her teachers allowed to find their own aides. All of this was done out of the superintendent's office. Some of her best teachers left to take jobs in other school systems; others came with a steady stream of complaints that their new paraprofessionals—Asians, Hispanics, African-Americans—were useless. "She yells at the kids," one teacher told Tedeschi, "and half the time I have no idea what she's talking about." "I asked him to discuss 'The Pit and the Pendulum' with the kids," another said of her new aide, "and he told me it was violent and not culturally relevant. Besides, what's a man doing working as a middle-school aide in the first place? I don't trust him."

Teachers also complained about the students who began to populate their classrooms, as Reilly closed the structurally unsafe inner-city schools and consolidated programs. "I can't control these kids anymore," Kitty Hitchcock announced at a teachers' meeting. "Some of them belong to gangs. The Asian kids will only talk to other Asian kids, and the kids who come together on the bus from downtown refuse to work with anyone who doesn't ride their bus." Hitchcock's comments started a gripe session that went on for the better part of an hour, during which Lucinda Valdez, who had been reassigned by Reilly when he closed the inner-city middle school to teach eighth-grade math at Elmore, exchanged glances quietly with two or three others who had recently joined the faculty.

As Tedeschi's problems grew, so did enrollments at the local private schools. As far as Reilly was concerned, this was just fine. The families were paying taxes anyway, and this left more open spaces for students from elsewhere in the system to be enrolled at Elmore.

Over the next five years, by tightly controlling the budget, Reilly was able to maintain enough of a margin of support on the school committee and in the county to continue his tactics. Despite threats from and fights with the teachers' union, he froze salaries and continued to do what he referred to as "cleaning house," that is, he found ways to dismiss teachers and administrators whose performance he judged to be less than optimal, or he squeezed them out by consolidating programs, reorganizing the school districts, and redistributing students from the now closed inner-city schools to the suburban schools. He instituted a merit pay system for teachers based on the performance of their students on standardized tests and enforced his strict rules of student discipline which were posted in large block letters all over the schools. From kindergarten through grade 12, students were required to walk single-file through hallways. Talking was not allowed. Students who arrived late found themselves locked out of classrooms, and parents were summoned immediately when students misbehaved. Teachers were ordered to double the amount of homework and use higher grading standards.

In addition to "cleaning house," Reilly began to shift some of the resources and some of the stronger teachers away from schools such as Tedeschi's and into the more ethnically diverse neighborhoods and vice versa. He actively recruited minority teachers and also proved successful at getting grant money to support programs and the purchase of new equipment.

Reilly's aggressive tactics got results. Attendance improved; more students stayed through graduation, with over 70 percent going on to college or to other forms of advanced education; and most striking, scores on standardized tests went from about average for the state to being near the top. By the end of Reilly's fifth year as superintendent, Marsh County was producing more Merit Scholars than any other county in the state. Reilly was named "educator of the year" by the governor and was honored in a special ceremony at the capitol, where he also received a letter of commendation from the President of the United States.

Despite the honors Reilly and his school system received, the relationship between Reilly and many of the administrators and teachers grew increasingly tense. On one occasion, Reilly walked into a classroom and accused a teacher of napping while the students read to themselves at their desks. "Get your things and get out," Reilly had told the teacher. "Don't come back tomorrow." The teacher, who had considerable seniority, filed a union grievance and was ordered reinstated. After that, Reilly made a point to check on him virtually to the point of harassment. At least three to four times a month, at irregular intervals, Reilly walked into the teacher's classroom unannounced.

While some of the parents virtually worshipped Reilly, most teachers and principals hated and feared him. They resented his constant intrusions into their classrooms, his admonitions to get tougher, and his barrage of rules and regulations. At the slightest hint of a problem with a student, teachers and principals were called to account, orally and in writing, for what had happened, how it had happened, and the remedial actions taken. If Reilly didn't like the remedies, he countermanded them, generally without telling the involved parties what he had done. So long as standardized test scores continued to improve and students continued to graduate, the school committee continued to uphold Reilly's actions. In the end, however, it was the teachers and principals who were able to swing the balance on the school committee and finally bring Reilly down.

Tedeschi and Reilly Go to War

Helen Tedeschi had disliked Bruno Reilly from the start, and things had gotten worse—much worse—over the years. Motivated by stories she had heard about Reilly, she had initially advised her friends on the school committee not to hire him, but they seemed to go out of their way to justify their actions. "Just give him time," one friend had told her, "and he'll get things moving around here. We think he's our man to do something about the kids from the city."

Reilly's illustrated lecture at the beginning of his contract and his unwillingness to discuss the changes he was mandating had confirmed Tedeschi's feelings. Not only did she feel he handled personnel issues poorly, she also believed that the improvements that were being made in the system had begun long before Reilly had appeared. In fact, Reilly had been brought in during the third year of a ten-year plan that had already included huge increases in the school budget; redistricting for more diversity; a teacher-training program; better teacher salaries; the use of specialists in math, science, reading, and learning disabilities; and the introduction of Head Start. Shortly after Reilly's arrival, however, teacher turnover increased and morale began to fall. A number of the older teachers became quite outspoken about feeling that they were just putting in their time until retirement.

"Some of the parents might think you're hot stuff," Tedeschi had yelled in exasperation at Reilly when he appeared in her office one day, "but we know better. All you're doing," she said, "is taking credit for what we've already started. You think you can make our ten-year plan happen in half the time, but the situation isn't as simple as that. You think that by dividing us up and using scare tactics, you're protected. Well, you're not, and I intend to do something about it."

"You don't care about education," Reilly shot back. "All you care about is yourself and your power. If someone supports you, you don't care if they can't teach for beans or even if they fall asleep in class. You and your buddies in the union have gone out of your way to protect bad teachers and maintain a mediocre system for as long as you can. I could really clean this place up if it weren't for people like you. Besides, you let your teachers use their students as guinea pigs. All this new stuff you do just doesn't work. Since I've been here," he added, "the other schools in the system have improved a lot more than yours! You had better shape up, or you'll be out of here, too."

"*I* don't care about education?" Tedeschi fumed. "Since you got here, the only thing our students have learned is how to take tests. Your whole ego is tied up in how well our students do on math tests. You don't care if they understand what they're doing just so long as they can memorize it and spew it back. It's only a matter of time," she said. "It's only a matter of time before people figure out just what a phony you really are."

Epilogue

Six months after Tedeschi and Reilly's argument, elections were held in Marsh County. Helen Tedeschi and several of her friends ran for school committee and won, finally edging out the Reilly supporters by a narrow margin, with voters from Elmore Township turning out in record numbers.

"People don't know what's good for them," Bruno Reilly had muttered to himself. He hadn't been surprised when the newly elected school board of Marsh County informed him they would not be renewing his contract, effectively firing him after six years with the school system. This had been his fifth school superintendency in a 26-year career; all had ended essentially the same way. Looking back, Reilly remained committed to both his educational tenets—a return to traditional values and highly structured systems—and to his methods for achieving these results, including firing nonperformers, basing pay on merit, and keeping tight controls over personnel and students alike.

QUESTIONS TO CONSIDER

1. Identify what you believe needed to be changed in the Marsh County School System prior to and during Reilly's superintendency. What do you think Reilly should have done differently to bring about these changes? How and why? What about Tedeschi?

2. How does this case reflect experiences you have had?

3. What do you believe the roles of a principal, superintendent, and school committee to be in managing the system of education?

4. What do you believe your rights and responsibilities are to a school system and its various stakeholders (students, parents, etc.) both in and out of the classroom?

5. The school committee is essentially the equivalent of a corporate board of directors and has a fiduciary responsibility to represent the best interests of the organization. Did the previous school committee (during Reilly's reign) act responsibly in supporting Reilly? Why? Did the new Marsh County school committee act responsibly in removing Reilly from his job? Why?

6. Was Reilly successful? Why? What about Tedeschi?

RECOMMENDED READINGS

French, J. R. P., & Raven, B. H. (1959). The bases of social power. In D. Cartwright (ed.), *Studies in social power.* Ann Arbor: University of Michigan Press, pp. 150–167.

This classic paper classifies and describes the various social powers that individuals may possess, use, and abuse in any given setting. This is particularly useful for understanding the ways in which the key case characters manipulate and change their environments to suit their needs.

Fullen, M. G., & Miles, M. B. (1992, June). Getting reform right: What works and what doesn't. *Phi Delta Kappan,* 73: 745–752.

This entire edition of *Phi Delta Kappan* is useful in promoting thinking about managing change in our school systems.

Kanter, R. M. (1983). *The change masters: Innovation for productivity in the American corporation.* New York: Simon & Schuster.

The corporate world, driven by the need for productivity, has had far greater impetus to learn to manage change than our tax-supported schools. As such, the corporate world has developed methods and insights into leadership of the management of change; most are highly applicable to educational settings.

Lewin, K. (1952). Group decisions and social change. In G. E. Swanson, T. M. Newcomb, & E. L. Hartley (eds.), *Readings in social psychology.* New York: Holt, Rinehart and Winston, pp. 459–474.

More than 30 years after Lewin formulated his process for the management of change in organizational settings, his model is still most often cited and used. Lewin details the reasons people resist change and suggests that for change to be effective, it most often must involve input from those who are affected.

London, M. (1988). *Change agents.* San Francisco: Jossey-Bass.

While this book was written for use by human resource professionals, it guides the reader through the analysis of the need for change, the evaluation of proposed changes, and techniques for implementation of change.